Al Lautenslager, a resident of Phoenix, Arizona, is an eight-time published, best-selling author, entrepreneur, book collector, businessperson, and professional speaker who is passionate about baseball. Currently, he is enjoying retirement, pursuing his passions for baseball, travel, writing and family life.

His passion for baseball has extended to his working as a Spring Training Usher for the Cincinnati Reds and Cleveland Guardians at Goodyear Ballpark.

Al's visits to ballpark, whether major or minor league, during his travels makes him the ultimate baseball fan.

At the beginning of *Baseball Confidential*, I mention the first professional baseball game that I attended. That was with my Dad. I will never ever forget it. He and I shared so much baseball together whether playing, going to games or coaching.

The relationship between father and son is no doubt strengthened through the love of baseball and that was definitely the case for my dad and me. We spent lots of positive time together, and I had a few life lessons along the way. I have a picture of my dad and me of the last ball game we attended together currently on my desk. I cherish that as well as the memories and lessons he provided for me. Saying thanks is an understatement but he is watching and guiding me from above. I miss you Dad and love you.

For all of that, I dedicate this book to my dad, Alfred J. Lautenslager. Yes, he and I share the same name so I am reminded of him continuously. Dad, I wish you could read this book and see that it was you that started my passion. Enjoy this dedication.

Al Lautenslager

BASEBALL CONFIDENTIAL

A Revealing Look at Behind the Scenes Communication Between Players, Coaches and Managers

AUSTIN MACAULEY PUBLISHERS™

LONDON • CAMBRIDGE • NEW YORK • SHARJAH

Ordering Information
Quantity sales: Special discounts are available on quantity purchases by corporations, associations, and others. For details, contact the publisher at the address below.

Publisher's Cataloging-in-Publication data
Lautenslager, Al
Baseball Confidential

ISBN 9798889105633 (Paperback)
ISBN 9798889105640 (ePub e-book)

Library of Congress Control Number: 2023913026

www.austinmacauley.com/us

First Published 2024
Austin Macauley Publishers LLC
40 Wall Street, 33rd Floor, Suite 3302
New York, NY 10005
USA

mail-usa@austinmacauley.com
+1 (646) 5125767

In this crazy world, acts of kindness are looked for and needed. I am a big proponent of these acts. Thanking people is one of those acts. I thank you as much as I can. There are so many instances that I can think of where thanks were imperative and many times still not enough. Thanking those in the effort of developing and producing *Baseball Confidential* is one of the instances.

First, as usual, my greatest thanks go to my wife, Julie. Her support, encouragement and love are never-ending and I am so appreciative and happy about that. Not only is she my rock, but she also shares my passion for baseball. Her knowledge is way beyond the average fan, and we love sharing stories, opinions and watching many many games together. She doesn't ask a lot of questions about the game, she answers many. I love you, Julie Ann.

Daughter Allison continues living her dream in the great outdoors, hiking, snowboarding, and living life in Oregon. Her support is also never-ending. Son Bradley continues to soar in the educational pursuit of his artistic passion and daughter Courtney continues to shine as a great mother. Their support is key, and I am appreciative of that. I love all three of you!

A big thank you goes out to all of the players, coaches, and managers that I interviewed. Each one was forthcoming, honest, and passionate about what they shared with me. They are all the epitome of professional baseball men, and I am honored to know them.

Little did I know that a passion that started when I was an 8-year-old playing baseball in the backyard, going to ball games and having a catch with my dad would lead to this book. I am grateful to all who have supported me in my journey. Thanks to all of you for allowing me to share and to be gratified. I look forward to more baseball and continuing my passion.

Lastly, animalistic support is still there. Nola and Ivy are always by my side in all that they do in their daily activity. They know I appreciate them and thank them. Just count their daily treats. And then, as always, there is Lu.

Table of Contents

Introduction: The Wonderment

I had just gone to my very first major league ball game at old Crosley Field in Cincinnati, Ohio. I didn't know what to expect but was surely very excited as I passed old 'Peanut Joe.'

Growing up in Cincinnati, Ohio, I still remember that game as it if was yesterday. I wore my little league uniform, and my rubber cleats. Absolutely, I took my mitt; the one that I oiled every night, that my dad ran over with the family car (purposefully) to break it in like a worn saddle. The Reds had the coolest uniforms, sleeveless, full of red (my favorite color) and white. The players appeared on the field, the organ shouted the Star-Spangled Banner, and the umpire yelled that infamous cadence, 'Play Ball!' Right then and with one more 'charge' fanfare, I knew I was hooked. I was one of the millions of young boys that stood at the imaginary plate, in the bottom of the ninth with two outs and a full count. Of course, I hit the game-winning, walk-off, home run with the unbelievable roar of a home-town crowd. We all had dreams. Dreams turned into passions and baseball was mine then and it is now.

It's worth it, as part of baseball lore, to just take a bit here, to talk about that baseball game icon that we all walked by and talked about all through our baseball days. 'Peanut Jim' Shelton was a fixture found outside of Reds games for 50 years, whether at Crosley Field or Riverfront Stadium in Cincinnati in later years. He'd stand at his roaster pushcart, decked out in his trademarked silk top hat, black frock coat and raggedy but presentable bowtie. He was proud when he looked you in the eyes and belted out, "Wanna bag of peanuts? Who wants peanuts?"

Peanut Jim *was* a Cincinnati fixture, with true Midwestern, all American values: hard working with a sense of belief, tradition, and tremendous pride. History tells that Peanut Jim was raised on his father's peanut farm in Union, South Carolina. With a traveling and entrepreneurial spirit, Peanut Jim visited Cincinnati in 1932, spent 75 cents on a roaster, and launched that notable hand-roasted peanut vending business.

Once past Peanut Jim, I was hit with that famous hot dog aroma, complete with yellow mustard and sometimes sauerkraut. Yes, ballpark franks have a very distinct smell that ingrains itself in your sensory brain forever. I can smell them even as I write this now.

When you got that whiff you had to find the nearest hot dog vendor walking the stands to make your traditional purchase.

I was a baseball kid. I was at the game. I had my glove and was in full uniform, but I knew there was nothing better than ballpark food. My friends and I consumed more than one hot dog each, washed that down with a cold Coke and still had room for popcorn, peanuts and probably another dog. Thank you, Dad!

Oh yeah, besides the gastronomic celebration there was a baseball game.

It was the summer of 1964; a warm Saturday and I remember the Cincinnati Reds were playing the Los Angeles Dodgers. Cincinnati utilized two pitchers in that game where they would eventually prove to be victorious in a 6-4 win over the west coast visitors. Those two Reds pitchers went on to become two of my favorites as I learned the game and became a true fan: yes, even at the age of eight. Jim O'Toole started the game, lasted seven innings and was relieved by left hander, Joe Nuxhall.

O'Toole went on to complete a ten-year major league career; nine with the Reds and his last season with the Chicago White Sox. Joe Nuxhall enjoyed success and became the Reds radio broadcaster. Nuxhall was a presence in radio broadcasting for the Reds that lasted over 40 years. He was well liked, a Cincinnati and later, an MLB icon and honored and revered all the way to the end. He was probably most remembered for having been the youngest player ever to appear in a Major League game, at the age of fifteen years, 316 days. I remember him because of his early pitching and the broadcasting of all the many games I listened to since.

All of that aside, I enjoyed the game so much that the memory still sticks in my mind after all these many years. I came away from that game an even bigger fan, a true eight-year-old ready to dive headfirst into baseball fandom and ready for many more years of baseball memories.

I understood most of what was going on, in between popcorn, peanuts, and hotdogs. One thing, though, baffled me, at my young age and caused me to wonder for a few years after that. That bewildering scenario happened later in the game around the fifth, sixth, and seventh inning. The catcher, who was Johnny Edwards, another favorite of mine (Johnny was my childhood nickname), would call time out and trot to the pitcher's mound. I thought, at that time, what are he and pitcher O'Toole talking about? Is he asking questions? Is he suggesting something to do? What were they talking about? I asked my dad at the time, who took me to the game, what that mound visit was all about and he told me that happens in baseball for many reasons leading to many types of conversation. I was perplexed, amazed and in wonderment all at the same time. I wanted to hear those conversations. I wanted it blasted over the ballpark loudspeaker system. Don't leave me, an eight-year-old fan, out in the dark about that interaction.

Here I am, many years later, often wondering and guessing what is said. I've seen many more mound visits since then but still have to guess and figure out what was said during those visits. Sometimes, the manager walked out to the mound along with the catcher and sometimes, he didn't. Sometimes, others joined in and sometimes others didn't. Was the conversation different or the same, each time?

This is one of many insides, baseball wonderments that exist. I found it time to find out more about those conversations. That all led me to wonder what managers say during different game situations, what is said during pre-game pep talks and post-game messages to teams. What do catchers say in the many different situations they get in to? I wanted to find out, so, after much research, talking to pitchers, catchers, players of all types, managers, and even umpires, I now have a better idea.

Mound visits don't rank high on the list of things that receive baseball attention. It's hard to get players, coaches, or managers to talk about them or share in their confidences. Fans don't like them much, but they do wonder about them. Baseball reporters will ignore them unless there is a popular or significant story line related.

Every fan wants to know what is said on the mound, in the locker room, behind closed doors and more. I am now here to reveal some of those confidences, write about them and to share those conversations with the many other fans who also may be in wonderment. I call it *Baseball Confidential*.

Respect

Written and Unwritten Rules

Two topics talked about when discussing player communication and mound visits, whether behind the scenes or out in the open, are trust between player, coach, pitcher and catcher, and respect. Respect generally is talked about as it relates to respecting the process and the people involved, especially, coaches and managers.

Major League Baseball has been around since 1869. Throughout the history of the league, we have seen plenty of players, teams, stadiums, ballparks, records, rule changes, and more change. One area that has stayed consistent over the lifetime of baseball is what is sometimes referred to as baseball's unwritten rules, an entire subculture of common practices. This subculture has been passed down from team to team, generation of players to the next as well as within the community of fans.

A lot of unwritten rules are there out of respect. Respect for the game, the field, the players, the opponents, coaches, and managers. We are talking mostly about respect between pitchers and coaches as it relates to mound visits. Respect for the game takes the form of things like, not admiring a home run, making a spectacle of it or displaying an in-your-face bat flip. When you hit a home run, you're supposed to act like you've hit one before.

Buck Showalter, manager of the New York Mets said, "You have to respect the game. The baseball gods will get you if you're not being true to the game."

Jackie Robinson preceded that respect statement by saying, "I'm not concerned with your liking or disliking me…all I ask is that you respect me as a human being."

Respect on the mound and in the clubhouse takes a few different forms.

Starting pitchers and reliever, all live by the same code of respect during a baseball game. For instance, if a manager comes out to bring in a bullpen pitcher, the pitcher to be replaced stays on the mound until the manager asks for the ball from him. It is an unwritten rule that pitchers should not walk off the pitcher's mound and off of the field, to the dugout until the manager gets to them and takes the ball. There have been times when a rookie will forget this and will get a talking to by the manager when they come back to the dugout.

Case in point: On a hot summer Friday night in Cincinnati, they were facing division foes, the St. Louis Cardinals. Pitching for St Louis was rookie pitcher Genesis Cabrera. Cabrera entered the game in the eighth inning and successfully retired the side. He returned to pitch the ninth inning for the Cardinals, with the Cardinals winning 7-3, up by four runs. Cabrera immediately allowed two straight singles as the ninth inning opened. Manager Marmol wanted to preserve a victory, so he did what many managers would do. He made a pitching change. As Marmol strolled to the mound and was almost there, Cabrera wound up and smashed the ball into the ground of the mound. It bounced upon impact and manager Marmol caught the rebound. Almost at the same time, he grabbed the revolting rookie player and proceeded to have a confrontational discussion, right in his face. You can bet respect was mentioned during that scold.

"Your ego can't get in the way of being a professional," Marmol later said. "I've known him (Cabrera) a long time. He'll be just fine. We have a good, veteran group that will address it. The kid's a competitor, he wants to be in there. You can't fault him for that."

Later, one of the more famous veterans of the team did in fact address it. Veteran slugger Albert Pujols spoke to Cabrera as the pitcher sat, with arms crossed, on the bench. It's not sure exactly what words were said but knowing the respect for Pujols and Cabrera being a fellow Dominican, you can bet his words of wisdom were heard.

Pujols finished, tapped Cabrera on the top of his cap and walked away. Lesson taught; lesson learned. *Baseball Confidential* or unwritten rules, the game still revolves around respect.

Trust is as much a key component as respect. The relationship and ensuing trust between a manager and a pitcher are both crucial for team success. The manager needs a strong, fundamentally sound pitcher; the pitcher needs a manager who trusts him and has confidence in him. That's the solution for the respect discussed previously.

The two must work together to win games. When the manager hands the ball to the pitcher, he is really telling him that he trusts him to have the game in his hands. When the pitcher falters, the manager takes the ball back, asking someone else to take the game in hand.

Another situation as told by Jason Turbow of The Baseball Codes was in a game between the Philadelphia Phillies and the San Francisco Giants. Kyle Kendrick was the pitcher on the mound. He pitched well into the sixth inning and his team was leading 5-1. That's a comfortable situation for a pitcher. Then things got rocky. Rocky can take many forms. Let your baseball imagination run wild.

A single was followed by a single was followed by a double. The result? A run for the Giants. Manager Ryne Sandberg had seen enough and made the mound visit that most managers would make at this point. Kendrick was very frustrated at what just happened. He took one look at Sandberg approaching the mound, realized what was about to happen and on his own, took off for the dugout. He blazed pass the approaching Sandberg, handing off the ball as he passed. Usually, the opposite situation exists as we will learn where the pitcher doesn't want to or even refuses to come out of a game.

A pitcher must wait for his manager to reach the mound, then hand him the ball before being dismissed and walking off of the mound. That will be discussed repeatedly here. We just discussed respect. Respect in this case would be waiting for the manager to reach the mound to make the pitching change, receive the ball and continue the process with the replaced pitcher walking off. Kendrick violated that respect according to what Turbow reported. No player should ever never show up or in this case, walk out on the manager in front of a stadium full of avid fans.

There are many more stories of pitcher's antics as it relates to the treatment of a manager during a mound visit. The bottom line is the game of baseball has unwritten rules, rules of respect and decorum, and honoring a manager's position with respect.

24

Pitchers and Catchers

Just Throw It in There – Pitcher Catcher Relationships

By now, you are understanding that pitching is as much a mindset and relationships as much as it is a physical accomplishment. Some pitchers deal with the mental part better than others. Some think that the pitcher's mound is a lonely place to be during a game. It can be even lonelier now that MLB rule changes are limiting the number of visits by a pitcher's friend to make it less lonely (and to potentially save game time).

Regardless of the mindset, regardless of the mechanics, most mound visits boil down to just a few fundamentals. Often said are things like, calm down and take a breather, let's figure out how to get out of this jammed situation, and here is a reset of the plan of attack for the next batter and the rest of the game, just like we do all season. Also, regardless of the mindset of the individuals involved, messages that are communicated have their own nuances. Many messages are tailored for just one person or situation and are, many times, unique. If a team has thirteen pitchers on staff, there are usually thirteen different approaches and messages. Few mound visits involve the mechanical things like arm angles, shoulder positioning, leg pumping or how to hold the baseball on certain pitches.

Telling a pitcher to relax is the thing that will cause them to not relax. That is why you see pitching coaches and catchers many times telling jokes or bringing humor into the conversation.

Coaches and catchers, both, read body language. That is discussed over and over when talking to any pitching coach, manager, or catcher. A lot can be read by watching expressions, movement, and other physical attributes. Eye contact, putting a hand on shoulder, understanding breathing motions are just a few of those language items that are monitored to gauge a pitcher.

Many coaches don't like to spend a lot of time talking about mechanics. Many think that is a between game fix, before or after, not a fix during the game. A coach's goal is to get players to the point where mound visits aren't as necessary every time a pitcher gets into a jam. It's important for a player sometimes to figure out their way out of situations on their own, self-adjusting in other words. Changes or no changes are then made or not made accordingly.

Scott Kapers, currently a catcher in the Texas Rangers minor league system was a former Class A Spokane Indians catcher. Scott was quoted by The *Spokesman-Review* (spokesman.com), the largest news and information provider in the Inland Northwest, based in Spokane, WA, reporting on the pitcher/catcher relationship, "When I was younger, it would be more like the pitcher is having a tough time or his body language is bad. As I got older, it was on me, and I kinda know when to walk out there." Kapers is a believer in mound visits working when made at the right time for the right reasons. He uses his visits to give a pitcher a break, many times from their timing or to distract them from a bad situation that just happened. He is right when he says, "They're all professional pitchers here. They know how to throw strikes. They've thrown so many times they know what they're doing." That seems to be a pervading approach by many MLB catchers today.

Relationships and Reasons to Visit

A lot of conversation in baseball, before, during and after a game depends on many different strategies, scenarios, planning and actual plays during the game. This all really boils down to three things: one is the pitcher, one is the catcher, and the other, which I'll lump as one, is strategies and tactics.

Many will say that the most important part of the game is pitching. With pitching comes a pitcher and a catcher. Each is integral and essential individually, as well as in tandem. Next time you are at a game, watch the pitcher and catcher. Usually, there is a vibe between the two, non-verbal communication and a true partnership in action. The relationship between the two boils down to trust. A pitcher delivers and executes. A catcher leads the pitcher as well as having responsibility for his position. A pitcher has to trust the leading that the catcher does whether in calling signals for certain types of pitches or the face-to-face communication on mound visits. Communication is key in all sports. Baseball is certainly no different. Greg Maddux, when pitching for the Atlanta Braves and Chicago Cubs needed to be synchronized with his catchers in order to execute the pitching just as he laid out in his pre-game plan. The pitcher-catcher relationship was crucial.

During my trips to spring training each year, I see rows of pitchers throwing to rows of catchers. I also see catchers doing a lot of talking, one on one counseling, lots of listening, all starting to build the necessary relationships needed for a successful season. Not only is there a lot of talking but there is a lot of listening. The catcher is getting in position to lead at this point. Look at recent baseball managers who were successful. They were former catchers. Bruce Bochy, David Ross, and Mike Matheny come to mind. They all are and were good at relationship building and being able to deal with the stresses of the season, games, the players, personalities and play by play.

That relationship is the key during the heat of battle in a game. At any level of baseball, you will see catchers call time out and trot out to the pitcher's mound for conversation, much like I saw (and questioned) in 1964 for the first time. Sometimes, these mound visits are called for by the manager and coaches but other and most times, the catcher decides when to visit. The catcher has a reason for the visit which will influence what is talked about, face to face, catcher to pitcher. The catcher decides all of that as part of his leadership. These days, there are different mound visit strategies employed with the advent of mound visit limitations and rule changes.

As Reported by Tim Kurkjian, *ESPN* Sportswriter, reporting on information from *ESPN* baseball analyst Bobby Valentine, there was an instance in late 2010/2011 where a pitcher maybe signed a playing contract with a particular ball club just because of the catcher and the ensuing relationship that would happen with that catcher. Cliff Lee joined former teammate Carlos Ruiz when he signed with the Philadelphia Phillies. Ruiz was known, especially to Lee to be a great defender, could throw guys out attempting to steal second and great at calling a ball game for his pitchers. Cliff Lee knew that in order for him to be effective, he had to be, as Kurkjian so well said, synchronized with his catcher in order to execute at a high-performance level, the pre-arranged pre-game plan.

Brent Mayne was a catcher for many teams but mostly the Kansas City Royals from 1990-2004. As *Wikipedia* states, 'the well-traveled Mayne was an effective catcher and an excellent handler of pitchers. He blocked the plate well and had a strong arm.'

As Kurkjian reported on Mayne, "Some pitchers need to be patted on the back, some need to be kicked in the ass, and a catcher has to have a feel for that. That's extremely important. A catcher has to be able to sense that. Catchers sometimes have to be an amateur psychologist in some ways. There's so much more to pitching than following a scouting report to a tee. That's not how it works." That's the kind of relationship mentioned earlier regarding pitcher Cliff Lee signing to re-join former teammate, catcher Carlos Ruiz.

Mayne continued in the report, "Anyone can sit in the stands and look at a scouting report and know what to throw next. But sitting in the stands, you can't see the subtle shift that the hitter makes after a pitch. Only the catcher can see that. And that's where the feel for the pitcher comes in. The best pitch any pitcher can throw is the one he can throw with conviction, whether it's the right pitch or the wrong pitch. The catcher's job is to give him that conviction." Making a mound visit to ensure this conviction and to suggest adjustments to a pitcher to achieve that are part of baseball strategy and catcher management of pitchers.

The question then becomes, when should a catcher make that decision to visit the pitcher and most of all, why? Both will determine the conversation.

Coach McCreary mentioned in an article, 'When should a Catcher Go to the Mound,' for Baseball by the *Yard* (coachesinsider.com) a few reasons for mound visits and when a catcher should make the visit. There are more than what is on the list that we will get into and expand upon, but here is his quick list of reasons or game scenarios:

Two quick outs. When a pitcher gets two outs in quick fashion in an inning, a catcher should remind a pitcher that the inning is not over. The message to the pitcher is one of bearing down and going right after the next hitter.

Good hitter/base open. Especially with two outs, a catcher should remind a pitcher what he can do with his pitching with first base open. Walking the guy isn't a problem because a worse hitter is up next.

Bullpen is up. When a pitcher gets up in the bullpen during a jam, it is a good idea to have a talk with the pitcher. It can settle him down which may allow him to pitch out of the jam and also give the guy in the pen more time to warm up.

Injury behaviors. If a catcher notices any unusual movements (shaking out the arm, squeezing the throwing hand often, unusual stretching, etc.), he should inquire if something is up. Hopefully, the coach will notice as well but a catcher should not assume that. If something doesn't look right, check it out.

Temper. If a pitcher shows signs that he is/has lost his composure, have a chat to settle him down. Don't let him pitch angry.

Hurt umpire. If the umpire gets hit with a wild pitch or foul ball, always take a slow trip to the mound, and talk to your pitcher. This gives the umpire a minute to regroup. He will LOVE you for it.

Stories will be shared throughout *Baseball Confidential* of real pitcher/catcher exchanges. In addition to Kurkjian's list, here are other reasons to add to the laundry list of why catchers would make mound visits:

Detecting a Flaw in Delivery. Pitchers are in a unique position to watch every pitch and every move by a pitcher, straight on. They catch these guys every day either in games or on the side. They know a pitcher's delivery intimately and can often detected flaws, even slight changes.

Changing Signs. More so in the days before pitchcom, pitchers would make mound visits to change signs that he used to signify certain pitches expected from the pitcher, especially if an opposing runner is on second base. This is not as common today with pitchcom, but it still happens.

Scouting Report Adjustments. Catchers know opposing hitters. There was probably discussion of opposing hitters in pre-game planning. A catcher will visit the pitcher to review a scouting report on a certain hitter and suggest a pitch sequence for him.

Tight Situations. Maybe there are bases loaded, no outs, and a powerhouse batter coming to the plate. A catcher will visit to remind a pitcher how to approach the situation, how to handle it mentally, and sometimes, just to give them a break in the action.

A Breather. Pitchers sometimes just need a break from the action, a breather. There are many stories, and we will relate some, where the break was given, and the pitcher came back in new form and succeeded above expectations.

Gauging Fatigue and a Mental State. We have already stated how well catchers know their pitchers. Regardless of how long a pitcher has been pitching, there are times where fatigue set in and affects pitching performance. Good catchers pick this up and visit the mound to talk about it. This is physical. The same can be said for mental approaches and mental fatigue. A good catcher knows when to break the game with a visit to address these.

Calm Down. Related to mental fatigue, pitchers can be caught in the moment and rush their process, whether it's between pitch routine or making the actual pitches. Catchers at times will go out to the mound and simply tell the pitcher to calm down, relax, and be deliberate. My favorite line for this is for the catcher to tell the pitcher, "Do what got you to the big leagues and don't worry about anything else." That can have a calming effect.

Slow Down. Related to a sense of calmness is the speed of the pitching process. Pitchers have been known to rush pitches. A casual suggestion of slowing down can work wonders for many pitchers.

Trips to the mound do not have to be very long. Drawing out a mound visits adds to the length of the game; not a desirable effect for anyone however doing whatever it takes to win is. Quick words can have a positive effect on a pitcher, whether a rookie or seasoned veteran. That's where a captain-like catcher comes in. That's necessary in today's game as much as knowing what to say. The same goes for pitching coach and manager mound visits.

A pitching coach will visit if a pitcher looks tired or even injured or for any other reason already listed. Sometimes, the pitching coach visit is triggered by the catcher, communicating to the coach that a pitcher needs a coach visit.

In the situations listed above, conversation between pitcher and catcher or coach resembles the following as reported by Roger Mooney of the *Tampa Bay Times* at the time:

Rays pitcher Jake Faria said former Tampa Bay Rays pitching coach Jim Hickey was short and direct during his visits.

"He'd say, 'What are you thinking here? Let's all be on the same page.' His visits were never long," Faria said. "It was really quick, 'Hey, what are you doing?' Boom, Gone."

Archer said former third baseman Evan Longoria would occasionally visit to remind him what to do if the ball is hit back to the mound.

"He'd say, the runner (on first) is slow, so you have a play at second," Archer said.

A pitcher who is struggling will often get a visit from a catcher or veteran infielder.

"Sometimes, a guy just needs a breather," Rays pitcher Jonny Venters said.

And sometimes, the situation calls for a little levity, humor, or a joke.

"I've gone to the mound and told a joke," Rays third baseman Matt Duffy said. "But not since I was in the minors." There is a whole Humor section within this book to learn more about this.

"Sometimes, I'll say, 'You scared? You nervous'?" Rays catcher Jesus Sucre said.

"They say, 'You kidding? I'm not scared'. I say, 'Okay, let's go'."

Faria recalled once hearing that former Angels shortstop Erick Aybar went to the mound when pitcher Jerome Williams was in a jam and asked Williams for the name of a good place to eat after the game.

These happen often in games with pitchers and catchers of all types. These are just a few examples and there are more in all of the stories within, here.

Insight from Pitcher – Eddie Guardado

A fan-favorite from the early 2000s Minnesota Twins teams, Eddie Guardado, was a pitcher for them from 1993 through 2003 (he then returned in 2008). Twelve of Guardado's 17 major-league seasons were spent playing for the Twins, and he added an extra four years as their bullpen coach. Eddies nickname is 'Everyday Eddie.' That moniker is a testament to his durable physicality and his long-time tenure in the Twins bullpen serving as a primary set-up man and many times, the team's closer. Everyday Eddie didn't literally pitch every day, but he pitched in a lot of games. To the casual fan and observer and even to opposing teams, it seemed like he did pitch every game. Many times, he would pitch on zero days' rest. If a pitcher can pitch with zero days' rest, they can be available every day. Eddie lived and worked for that availability.

One of the situations that *Baseball Confidential* is digging into is the communication between catcher and pitcher in pressure packed situations. Two base runners in a tight game is one of those pressure packed situations. Eddie was pitching. It was late in the game, the seventh or eighth inning. Up to the plate comes hard hitting Edgar Martinez batting for the Seattle Mariners. Everybody, especially Eddie Guardado knew of Edgar and what he could do.

Martinez was known as a force to be reckoned with. A Hall of Famer, he played for the Seattle Marines from 1987 to 2004 and was their hitting coach from 2015-2018. Guardado, nor anyone knew that Martinez would go on to finish his career as one of only six players in history with at least 300 homers, 500 doubles, a career batting average of at least.300, a career OBP of at least.400 and a career slugging percentage of at least.500 along with being a seven-time MLB All-Star, five-time Silver Slugger, and two-time batting champion. Edgar Martinez was inspired to play baseball after watching fellow Puerto Rican Roberto Clemente play in the 1971, World Series. Not a lot of ballplayers get a ballpark concession stand named after them. Today, you can visit 'Edgar's Cantina' at Safeco Field. Enough about Edgar but put all that behind a late inning at bat in a high-pressure situation against pitcher, Eddie Guardado.

When Martinez came to bat, it was an event and maybe a bigger event to be; it was electric and there was always a buzz in the stands, whether home or away. He truly was the best hitter of the time. Guardado proceeded with his pitch sequence. Martinez proceeded to hit foul ball after foul ball. That's not bad for a pitcher but the count did get to 3-2, a full count. More foul balls. So far, it was an eight pitch at bat. Terry Steinbach was the catcher for Guardado. Steinbach was a three-time All-Star player, won the 1988 All-Star Game MVP Award and caught two no-hitters during his career. He certainly knew his craft and would be a good compatriot to have a conversation with a pitcher in a pressure packed situation. Guardado felt that pressure. What's a good catcher to do? Call time out, venture out to the mound and have a conversation. In the spirit of *Baseball Confidential*, let's dig into what is said in that situation. We as fans can always guess but Guardado explained it in detail. Steinbach arrived at the mound, looked Guardado in the eye and before the catcher could start to impart his wisdom,

Eddie, the pitcher, out of answers almost asked catcher Steinbach, "What do you have?" This was his attempt to ask what pitch Steinbach could suggest at this point in the at bat.

Steinbach replied back to pitcher Eddie, "We are throwing the kitchen sink (many different types of pitches), at him and he is still fouling off pitches. Do you have anything (pitches) in your back pocket that we could use in this situation?"

Of course, Guardado, replied with, "I wish I did," He repeated the same thing wishing he did while wondering what to do next. That's a perfect example of situations that cause the mound visits we are talking about here. The at-bat was getting longer. The batter was pleased with hanging in there and the pitcher was frustrated because the batter was hanging in there.

It was almost epiphany like when Steinbach next spoke. He said to Guardado, "I have an idea. I'll tell you what we are going to do." Guardado, of course, was all ears at that point. Catcher Steinbach told pitcher Guardado that he was going to set up right down the middle and that Guardado was to cut the plate in half with a hard fastball. That certainly wasn't the strategy Guardado thought would work and he was surprised that Steinbach would suggest such a pitch to one of the best hitters in the game at that time.

Guardado even asked Steinbach at that time, "Is that the best idea you have? Right down the middle? We are talking about Edgar Martinez here." Steinbach sheepishly laughed and asked the pitcher what else he wanted to do, realizing options were limited.

Steinbach suggested, "Let's take a chance!"

Steinbach retreated back to his catching position, got into the proverbial catcher's crouch knowing it was a full count on the powerhouse batter. Pitcher Guardado threw the best, down the middle, splitting the plate in half pitch that he had ever thrown, fearing it was about to get smacked out of the park for a home run. That didn't happen. Edgar Martinez swung right through the pitch for strike three. The inning was over. Guardado said many, many 'Holy _____' after that pitch and was amazed that Martinez swung right through the pitch.

Guardado later asked catcher Steinbach if he noticed something in the batter's approach or swing at that moment. Steinbach said no. His rationale for the suggestion was that batters like Martinez and pitchers pitching to him are always looking for and at pitches that are in and out, breaking to one side or another, never right down the middle. When a pitch came right down the middle in the perfect spot, in a split second, Martinez got excited, and at the same time probably couldn't believe that he was getting the perfect pitch to hit and he swung through it. He didn't see the left-side or right-side breaking ball that he was expecting. Steinbach's suggested strategy worked. One never knows what's going to happen with a pitch. Sometimes, batters guess right and sometimes, they don't. That's the same with the average fan. They try to guess the next pitch type and sometimes are right and other times they are wrong. That's baseball and that's why Guardado got away with the classic pitch he threw.

The Guardado/Steinbach exchange is one type of conversation in the game: strategic but very much in the moment.

Guardado continued with what seemed to be everyday pitching. Sometimes, Guardado would pitch often to catcher AJ Pierzynski.

AJ Pierzynski played in Major League Baseball with many teams, mostly with the Minnesota Twins and Chicago White Sox. It turned out that Pierzynski is one of only ten catchers in Major League history to reach 2,000 hits in his career. AJ has caught no hitters and perfect games and knows how to approach pitchers in those critical mound visits. That came in handy with Eddie Guardado on the mound.

Many times, Pierzynski would approach Guardado, and point blank ask him, when he got to the mound, "What are you doing? Let's go and get it in gear. I want to go home. I want to see my wife and kids and you're holding things up". Pierzynski's' approach was to give the pitcher a breather, a chance to break up the pressure of the moment and sometimes, to maybe even have a little laugh to cut through the gravity of the situation.

As said, many times fans and others are wondering what is being talked about during the mound visit. Sometimes, it's not complicated. Guardado admitted that fans would be amazed at what's talked about like AJ Pierzynski begging to go home, wanting to go get something to eat or to motivate the pitcher to get his job done in the right way. Guardado stated that it's not always conversation about making adjustments or tweaks or discussing pitching mechanics. Catchers sometimes just need to break things up, take the pressure off at the moment, smile a little, laugh a little and just get back to making things fun. There are even times when there are comments about something or someone a pitcher or catcher sees with fans in the stands but that's not as often. Guardado did point out that ballplayers know they are just grown men playing a kid's game at least from a fun perspective.

Managers

Non-Pitcher Perspective – Insight from Marty Cordova

We have all seen different management styles either in the workplace or on the baseball field. Baseball managers are all different. They all have their different styles of management. You can judge whether they are right or wrong but, in the end, you usually judge by results.

Baseball management styles differ, as stated. Most are positive, motivating and focused on personal development among the everyday game management duties, strategies, and tactics. Some styles are not as positive.

Not every communication between player and manager is all rah-rah, rosy, peachy, and positively motivating. Some of that negative conversation is a particular manager's way of managing, right, wrong, or indifferent. Somewhere along the way, a manager may have learned that to get people to do something different you have to put fear into them or play with their feelings to the point where they get mad and end up performing. That's not the most popular way of managing, especially with ball players and especially in today's times but it has happened and still happens today.

We have discussed a lot of communication between pitchers, catchers, and managers. Hearing from a non-pitcher widens the perspective and provides more into that one-on-one player manager communication. Since the title of this book is *Baseball Confidential*, we are going to go behind the scenes on this one.

Martin Cordova is a former professional baseball left fielder who played in Major League Baseball mostly for the Minnesota Twins. In 1995, he was awarded the Rookie of the Year award from Major League Baseball.

Marty was known as hard-nosed player, intense and focused, always the first to the ballpark and last to leave, devoting countless hours to getting/staying in shape, healthy dieting, baseball fundamentals and always trying to improve his craft.

I first asked Marty to share any interesting, memorable pep talks or pre-game coach speeches he heard in his major league experience. He was quick to state that there really weren't any speeches before games. This was a common response from many players. Managers approached that whole topic with the attitude that players are mature adults and know why they are in the big leagues. They know what to do and have been coached on process, fundamentals, and routine. Post-game speeches were a different story. He did recount teams hearing a loud manager after a game that was lost, lacked fundamentals, or had its share of mistakes.

He did share detailed stories of managerial communication with players, most specifically his own situations.

These stories are not the typical motivating communication between manager and player but come with more of a different management approach involving fear, intimidation and sometimes embarrassment.

The manager in this case is Tom Kelly.

Tom Kelly is a former professional baseball player, coach, and manager. Over sixteen seasons, as the manager of the Minnesota Twins of Major League Baseball, he won two World Series championships.

Marty Cordova, playing for the Twins, says that Tom Kelly was a great guy but a 'hardnosed' manager that liked to test a player's mettle, grit, and determination.

We're talking about communication on the field, behind the scenes, between player and coach mostly. In talking with Marty Cordova, he shared, what he states as what goes on in the field in the moment. These two stories illustrate just that.

Marty's Twins were playing the Kansas City Royals. Terry Crowley, hitting coach for the Twins from 1991 through 1998, was watching from the sidelines for this at bat by Cordova. Tom Kelly was the manager. We've already stated that Kelly liked to manage by fear and embarrassment even though that didn't always work, at least for almost every other player. It didn't, admittedly, work for Cordova; however, he put up with it and figured out a way to deal with it. Marty Cordova preferred encouragement, extra hard work, but not embarrassment. He was not a fan of Kelly's approach of trying to motivate players by shaming them.

In this particular at-bat for Cordova, it was the eighth inning. The Twins had a runner on second base and the team was down by one run. The Royals brought in a known relief pitcher into the game. Relief pitchers always represent fresh opportunities. The batting team also had a fresh opportunity at the same time.

At the time of the pitching change, as the reliever was going through his warm-up pitches, Cordova went to the bench to consult with hitting coach Crowley. Cordova simply asked Crowley what his thoughts were on facing the new, incoming pitcher. The scouting report told them both that the reliever had, in baseball terms, a nasty slider pitch, many times unhittable. The conversations ensued into a conclusion between the two to sit on the slider, especially since the scouting report also indicated that a slider was pitch this pitcher threw 80% of the time. Hitting coach Crowley said come up with your strategy/plan and go for it. (Sitting on the slider means to wait until he, the batter, sees or suspects that pitch, the slider being pitched to the batter). With the strategy set, Cordova was ready to face the new pitcher…until, manager Tom Kelly jumped into the conversation (butting in and eavesdropping are descriptions that come to mind).

Tom Kelly's message, in his own style, was as follows: "Hey, Marty? You want to 'Sit' on a slider? Why would you wait for a pitch, sit on it, that you can't even hit." Kelly went on to fume to Cordova, that the pitcher could even tell him that particular pitch was being pitched and according to Kelly, Cordova still couldn't hit it. Kelly asked why Cordova, the waiting batter, would sit on a pitch that he couldn't hit. Of course, you can imagine the feeling and response from player Cordova (expletives deleted here). Cordova was irate that his manager would talk to a player like that.

At any rate, Cordova approached the at-bat, ready to hit, fuming with his manager's motivation (or lack of). The first pitch was outside and called a ball. The second pitch was the expected slider that the batter was 'sitting' on. Cordova let loose with a power swing and hit the ball cleanly to left field, for a base hit. The runner on third scored, the throw from left field came into no avail and Cordova darted to second base.

Cordova describes this as one of the more exciting and exhilarating moments in his baseball career. He looked back into the dugout and was eye to eye with his manager, in a classic, 'I told you so…' moment. Did Kelly think he was motivating his player with the negative talk? If he did, it worked, but the player was still fuming then and after for a long time.

Communication between player and manager happens every day, good or bad. There were no pep talks. In Tom Kelly's position, it was embarrassment, harassment, and fear-based communication. That continued during Cordova's career.

In another instance, Marty Cordova arrived at the ballpark one game day. Marty was always at the field early, the first one there and last to leave. He was known as being really dedicated to playing.

Manager, Tom Kelly, was there on this particular game day. Tom was typically an early riser and also early to the ballpark. Marty walked past Tom's office upon arriving to the clubhouse locker room, casually greeted him and made his way to his locker. Hanging on Cordova's locker was a handwritten note that simply stated: 'Marty Cordova vs. Justin Thompson. 0 for 12 with 8 strike outs. Good effin' luck. Ha.' Justin Thompson was the starting, opposing pitch that day. Again, Cordova was perplexed and frustrated with this management style, lacking any motivation but embarrassment.

It was game time and Cordova had a bad game. Trying hard, he struck out three times. Manager, Tom Kelly called Marty into his office after the game and told him, point blank, that he was not going to be playing in the next three days of games. Kelly's words, according to Cordova were, "You're going to come here to the ballpark, at 1 o'clock each day and we are going to hit extra batting practice, watch each game that follows and follow that with taking extra batting practice after the game. You're going to 'get right,' and when we, the team, goes to Seattle on the next road trip, you're going to play." Again, Cordova's irate feeling pegged the meter. He processed irate feelings well because he had to. He couldn't change managers. Cordova was one of those players that processed points like this. It was his decision to be cooperative and just do his best, regardless of management intimidation or tactics. That got him through each management approach and interaction with Kelly.

On that first day of the imposed extra batting practice, Cordova showed up promptly at 1 o'clock (probably showed up earlier, knowing his punctuality habits). He walked into the Metrodome, it was very cold as temperature was controlled as if the stadium was full of people exchanging body heat. There was not one person in the Metrodome at that time except maybe a few cleaning people. The batting practice cage was set up and ready. Tom Kelly showed up ready to throw batting practice.

Kelly was a lefty and actually was good at throwing batting practice. He threw hard; just what the player wanted and needed. He wasn't just throwing lobs to crank out automatically.

Cordova was finally getting warmed up and getting loose. Hitting Coach, Terry Crowley was standing behind the batting practice cage watching Tom Kelly fire pitches to batter Cordova.

The first practice pitch came, Cordova swung late and hit a foul ball directly it into the batting cage. Kelly threw the next pitch. Batter Cordova considered his swing to be late and fouled the ball again. Manager Kelly was not happy. He looked at Cordova with hands on hips with Cordova yelling at that moment, "Throw it." Kelly stopped. He told Cordova to come to the mound where he was standing. Before that, Cordova turned to Crowley behind the hitting cage and expressed his frustrations and that he didn't think he could handle the stress peacefully. He indicated he wasn't in the mood for negative management and negative motivation. Coach Crowley surely thought to himself that this could get ugly. Kelly, with his hands on his hips and a cigar in his mouth, said at that moment to Cordova, "This is what I want you to do. Walk up those stairs, go into the locker room, take your uniform off, fold it up nice and neat put it into your locker and retire. Do yourself a favor, do me a favor, do your family a favor and do the city and world a favor and retire from baseball. I'm sick of watching you play. I'm sick of looking at you. I'm sick of hearing about you. I'm sick of everything about you. (Marty, not a fighter was tempted at that point to change that notion)."

Despite the order, Cordova went back to the batting cage, hoping that cooler heads could prevail. Kelly threw the next pitch and Cordova launched a long a home run. Tom Kelly puts his hands out and said, "See," like he did something spectacular in the world of player motivation. As Cordova hit (successfully) more, he was told to put his heart into it. So, the manager's hitting advice was to put his heart into it after the player was just told to retire from baseball. Cordova's activity and work turned in to what amounted to an angry round of batting practice and it ended up being semi-productive according to Cordova.

This planned batting practice ritual went on for three days. The team went to Seattle for their away game series, playing in the Seattle Kingdome. Cordova's first day back in the playing lineup. His demeanor was still respectful but still fuming. Cordova stated that manager Tom Kelly and he loved each other in the wrong way. 'I have respect for him now. We just didn't like each other then or his management style didn't mesh with what I as a player needed or wanted.' Kelly thought Cordova could be a great player and he thought he could motivate him (in his own savage ways). Cordova's second at bat resulted in a rocket home run. As he rounded the bases, still steaming mad, all he thought about was this was the best 'I told you so,' moment, ever.

Now, a description of the rest of the story and more of what's remembered most.

The homerun was hit, the runner (Cordova) rounded the bases, stepped on home plate and was ready for the dugout receiving line to deliver high fives of congratulations. Cordova gave hitting coach Crowley a high five. Manager Tom Kelly tried to give him a high five and Cordova ducked under his attempt, to avoid him. In doing so, he accidentally couldn't get his hand up in time to give Pitching Coach, Dick Such a high five. Cordova then went down the rest of the line of high fiving players. Subsequentially, Cordova observed Tom Kelly at the end of the bench for the whole game, with what could be considered steam coming out of his ears. Kelly was very mad. The Twins lost the game 5-4 but that wasn't what Kelly was fuming about. In the locker room, after the game, Kelly came running up to Marty like he was ready to fight. He said (according to Cordova), "Listen you SOB, I don't care if you don't like me, Coach Dick Such is pulling for you, and you go around me and miss and ignore Dick Such. He cares about you, and you treat him that way?" Marty Cordova didn't say anything at that point still in a very defensive mode.

Marty understood that the pressures and tension were part of the job. He knew where Kelly was coming from, but Cordova still wanted to maintain his own self-respect. He knew it was his family that got embarrassed when he played poorly or that fans got upset when he struck out. He didn't think the manager considered those pressures.

That's the case with every player. Piling on with negative management approaches do not work with players like Marty Cordova but they happen. That's baseball. It works with some people, but others would end their careers because of that approach used on them. They couldn't take it. Tom Kelly thought he was weeding out the weak people. He probably was but he also was creating other problems that would affect team and individual performance. Marty Cordova stated that he knew Kelly's intentions were to get the best out of players

There have been many managers in baseball history with questionable management and coaching styles. Many managers like to test mettle, grit, and determination. Many kept their management jobs despite uproars, conflict, and dissension in the clubhouse or on the field with players, based on their approaches.

A manager's job is to keep his players together as a cohesive unit/team. There are many tactics to do this, but Tom Kelly did it his way. It's ok to be passionate and sometimes emotional but there are still fundamentals of management and people development to consider.

Successful managers usually have a good bond and rapport with players. The more successful teams win because the manager has the support of their players because of this rapport. This is one thing that has led teams, today, to hire younger managers, regardless of experience. The emphasis is communication between player and coach (Manager). That translates into a job to create a winning atmosphere giving players and teams a chance to win.

Did Tom Kelly do this? According to Marty Cordova, Tom had his own style, and it wasn't always favorable according to players.

Everybody processes management by fear in different ways. Many players experience fear or anxiety going into a game whether self-imposed or one imposed by an intimidating manager. High-level baseball players like Marty Cordova managed by how he interpreted and utilized that fear. Working through any fear is often the best path toward improvement and eventual success. That's what Marty Cordova did. Some players are motivated by that, and some shut down. Tom Kelly didn't care. It was his way. One additional point about confidential communication and rapport with players is Tom Kelly's relationship and approach with Hall of Fame player David Ortiz.

Former Minnesota Twin, and Hall of Famer, David Ortiz has written his memoir entitled, *Papi: My Story*. The whole second chapter of the book entitled, 'Tom Kelly and Me' is all about how much the renowned Twins manager negatively impacted player, David Ortiz, with his management style.

David Ortiz talks in his book about a particular game where manager Tom Kelly thought the team's play in the field was sloppy and haphazard. Because of that, he ordered all players to take fielding practice after the game. Ortiz's and other players thoughts were that that was something not done in major league baseball, not a mature approach to coaching or management. Ortiz hadn't seen that type of order before that time and hasn't seen it since. That was Tom Kelly's style whether players liked it or not.

A good baseball manager has to consider all aspects of a player: his health, his opponents, team morale and skills when considering and managing line ups. Did Tom Kelly do that? I'm not sure, but in our attempt here to uncover *Baseball Confidential*, it appears that his method and approach was just different.

That's how Tom Kelly managed. He managed everyone that way. Players hated him at one time or another but as time went on, some players admitted that it made sense; it was a different style and not one they would adopt but they understand Tom Kelly now.

Casey Stengel – Classic and Confidential

No baseball book that contains any stories would be complete without a mention or a story or two or three about the legendary Casey Stengel. Stengel is best known for managing the New York Yankees to ten American League pennants and seven World Series championships from 1949 to 1960. Casey's baseball career spanned over half a century. Of his seven World Series championships, he won five consecutive crowns (1949-1953), the only time that has been achieved. He was classified as the most dominant manager of any single decade in baseball history. Stengel was referred to as baseball's clown genius, known for his long-winded babbling double-talk and somewhat comedic talent and approaches. This carried over, at times to mound visits when conferring with his pitchers.

Those conferences range from simple to funny.

Casey Stengel spent time managing the New York Mets. Many baseball sources report that one of his pitchers, Roger Craig, recalled, "I was pitching one day and all of a sudden I kinda lost my control."

Casey walked to the mound and said to Craig, "Mr. Craig, what seems to be the trouble?"

Craig replied, "The ball feels really slippery."

Stengel reached down, said in his most matter-of-fact voice, to Craig, "Well, there's one ton of dirt below your feet. You might want to reach down and rub the blasted ball up." Casey then deliberately walked off of the mound. Mound visit over.

That same pitcher Craig talks about the time his Mets manager, Stengel, visited the mound to chat. Willie McCovey was coming up to bat. That alone signaled it was time for a mound visit. Stengel asked Craig, "Where do you want to pitch him? Upper deck or lower deck?" It sounds funny but Stengel got his point across with that approach.

On a hot, sunny July 4th Holiday game in 1934, Casey Stengel, then managing for the Brooklyn Dodgers made a mound visit during a game with the Philadelphia Phillies. This one was memorable for Stengel, the pitcher and all who witnessed the incident.

Pitching for the Dodgers was Boom-Boom (Walter) Beck. Beck didn't just have one of the more colorful nicknames in baseball history, he also had one of the sport's longest careers, pitching for 26 seasons, a true marathon run.

Stengel went to the mound to remove Beck from the game. The game was being played in Philadelphia's Baker Bowl, home to the Philadelphia Phillies from 1887 until 1938.

Beck was frustrated, fed-up and one of those pitchers who did not like being taken out of the game, no matter how bad his performance was. Once Beck knew of Casey's move, he turned and launched a long, hard throw to right field. Right field consisted of a 40-feet high wall made of tin. At the wall, the right fielder was Hack Wilson. He actually was leaning on the wall. Wilson had a 58 homerun, 191 RBI year, four years earlier. Wilson was known as being combative along with excessive alcohol consumption making him one of the most colorful sports personalities of his era. No one knows if he was still inebriated or hungover that day, but when he heard Beck's throw hitting the tin wall, not paying attention to exactly all that was going on, heard the ball, retrieved it and fired a strike throw to second base – all believing the ball was in play. Beck couldn't figure out the crowd chants that were more cheers. He soon realized the sense of his error and bowed his head. From their dugout, the opposing Phillies broke into gut-busting laughter. You can thank Stengel's mound management for that Baker Bowl highlight.

During Stengel's New York Mets tenure, he made frequent visits to mounds. He was a true coach but many mound visits were rarely motivational compared to trips to remove the pitcher.

Pitching for the Mets on one particular day was Tug McGraw. McGraw was a relief pitcher and long-time Major League Baseball player, pitching almost 20 years for both the New York Mets and Philadelphia Phillies.

Stengel approached the mound and immediately McGraw fired the first shot and told Stengel, "I'm not tired."

Stengel in his own managerial style replied back, "Well, I'm tired of you. People up there (pointing to the stands) are beginning to talk."

McGraw still pushed back, protesting his removal. He asked to pitch to one more batter. His rationale back to Stengel was, "But I got this guy out last time I faced him."

That created a classic mound visit conclusion by Stengel when he told McGraw, "I know, but it was in the same inning." McGraw obviously did not have a good negotiation hand when dealing with Stengel.

Finally, still with the Mets, Stengel approached the mound to talk with pitcher Larry Bearnarth, a New York native. There were two on, no outs, and future Hall of Famer, Orlando Cepada was up to bat next. Cepada, at that time was a feared batter. The situation called for a mound visit by Stengel. It was short and sweet. He went to the mound, looked right at Bearnarth and all he said was. "Tra-La-La." Who knows what that meant at that point in time? Stengel said it and turned around and walked off of the mound. Bearnarth was puzzled but continued to pitch. Bearnarth threw the ball, power hitter Cepada grounded into a rare triple play to end the inning. Bearnarth, relieved, walked to the dugout and found Stengel. It was at that point that he asked Stengel what he meant by, 'tra-la-la?' Casey's reply was staccato like and to the point. He told Bearnarth it meant, 'Triple Play.' That was a classic case of making the story fit the situation. That's Casey Stengel. That's baseball and that's a little bit of Casey Stengel, confidential.

Pitchers

Dennis Rasmussen – Pitcher and Coach Perspective

In this book, Umpire Al Clark shared a story about overhearing an Art Fowler conversation with the Oakland pitcher on the mound during that particular game. Art's comments to the pitcher were a warning that they had better get an out because, manager Billy Martin was getting pissed.

The same type of story was shared by Dennis Rasmussen, pitcher for the Yankees at the time of this reported incident. Rasmussen was a tall, left-handed pitcher that pitched for many teams during his MLB career including the Yankees. Talking to him results in lots of conversation and stories about big names of baseball past that he played with.

In 1985, Dennis was playing for Yogi Berra who ended up getting released sixteen games into the season. In comes replacement manager Billy Martin. For the record, according to Dennis, Billy did not especially like pitchers. If the game could be played, which it can't, without pitchers, Billy would have been a happier manager. Based on that, he certainly didn't favor Rasmussen. Dennis called it being on Billy's hit list and in line for Billy's wrath; however, Rasmussen was one of the younger players, not considered to be a big money player. Billy's wrath was usually saved more for the big free agents who got the wrath when things didn't go well.

It was Rasmussen's second year in the big leagues. Billy took over and Rasmussen was not having a great pitching year. Art Fowler that we were introduced to when talking with Umpire Al Clark was the pitching coach for Billy at this time. In this particular game, Art had already made two mound visits. He made a third. He didn't say anything until he got right on top of the mound and was face to face with the pitcher (Rasmussen in this case). He proceeded to tell Rasmussen, "This is the last time I'm coming out here. You're pissing Billy off. You better get somebody out." Rasmussen reported that Fowler said the same thing and blamed Billy on each visit. Based on this and the observations by umpire Al Clark, this seemed to be Fowler's standard modus operandi with nothing more creative.

Rasmussen got out of trouble after the first two visits but not after the third and was removed from the game. Rasmussen walked off the mound, shaking his head and was wondering the whole time if that was his pitching coach's (Fowler) only coaching message.

Fans are always wondering if mound visits result in automatic replacements of pitchers. Some managers do that and are predictable and others have conversations that may result in the pitcher staying put. I asked Dennis Rasmussen if he ever encountered a manager or pitching coach on the mound and talked him out of replacing him or pushed back to the point where he remained in the game. He did say he witnessed this happening one time, but he was not the one responsible for him staying in the game. He was not the one that pushed back. Mike O'Berry, the Yankees backup catcher at the time was the player behind the decision to leave Rasmussen in the game. The Yankees were facing the Baltimore Orioles at Yankee Stadium. Rasmussen was pitching in the eighth inning trying to hold a 2-1 lead for the Yankees. He was pitching well up to that point. Up to the plate came the heart of the Orioles lineup about to go head-to-head with Rasmussen. From a manager's perspective, the worst or close to the worst, happened. Rasmussen gave up a bunt hit, then an infield hit before getting the first out. Rasmussen then walked the next batter. Bases were loaded and there were two outs. Every pitcher who has ever been in that situation would tell the manager to leave him in. He could get the last guy out. That's just the way pitchers are wired. Managers then are faced with a decision. In this case, the Yankees had a pitcher warming up in the bullpen after Rasmussen walked the Oriole player and that bullpen pitcher was already at the peak of his warmth and was ready to enter the game.

There wasn't actually a mound visit that ensued. Rasmussen knew he was on shaky ground with what he had just given up. Looking into the dugout, Yogi Berra, manager at the time, looked like he was about to make a mound visit, probably to replace the pitcher. Catcher, Mike O'Berry also saw that Yogi was about to ascend the dugout steps to make his way to the pitcher's mound. (It took Yogi just a tad bit of extra time for that ascension given his height and the verticality of the dugout steps). Catcher O'Berry then hollered over to the dugout and waved Yogi back. He signaled for Yogi to stay put and not to visit the mound for a change. The pitching coach at the time, Mark Connor, noticed this and heard his catcher adamantly make his case and he grabbed Yogi before he went up those steps, telling Yogi to leave the pitcher in. The catcher was persuasive with his conviction that the pitcher should remain and could get through the situation at hand. Yogi's decision was to let Rasmussen continue pitching. The worst then happened. Rasmussen gave up a grand slam to the Oriole batter, Gary Roenicke. He now was the pitcher of a game where the opponents now led 5-2. The 2-1 lead evaporated with one swing. The catcher won his case to keep the pitcher in the game but only for what ended up being one pitch too many. Who knows what famous Yogi quote came from that?

There is one more note about that grand slam that is worth mentioning. The visiting Orioles had a fan contest every game where a fan's name was assigned to each batter of a particular inning. In this case, a local Baltimore area secretary who rarely watched baseball was the selected fan for batter Gary Roenicke. If that hitter hit a grand slam home run, the selected fan got one million dollars prize money. Roenicke delivered for the fan. He hit the grand slam homerun. Rasmussen's, 'one too many' pitch resulted in a windfall win for a non-suspecting fan.

Fast forward to today. Rasmussen is now the pitching coach for the Bluefield Ridge Runners, a summer collegiate baseball team of the Appalachian League. Rasmussen is now the one making mound visits and partaking in the art of coach/pitcher communication.

He tells of his mound visits, and they sound like many that we are hearing about. When he makes a mound visit, he is usually intent to break up some kind of monotony or pattern in the game as he describes it. Sure, there are times where the pitcher is not throwing well, or the other team has amped up their swings and messages might change. He indicated that you have to pick and choose your messages depending on the situation.

Sometimes, he views the game, the situation, sits back and waits a little longer than normal for a visit to see if the pitcher can figure out, within a few pitches, his way out of a predicament. Rasmussen states that baseball is a game of adjustments. Adjustments need to be made from pitch to pitch. He says it best by saying that sometimes, if not all the time, a pitcher has to be his own pitching coach. This is especially true in the big leagues where adjustments have to be made pitch to pitch, continuously.

Dennis Rasmussen will further use this as a coaching point, sometimes to the point of letting a pitcher go too long in a situation. His thought is a question of how a pitcher can learn to get out of trouble if they don't encounter trouble. In today's game, pitchers are removed before something bad happens. He also knows he is in a developmental role in the league that he is in now. He is clear to profess that he learned to get out of trouble himself because he got into his share of trouble and figure out a clear path forward.

Rasmussen has been on both sides. The pitcher being communicated to and now the coach communicating to the pitcher. Both offer different perspectives, and his stories share that. That's baseball!

Jack McDowell – Pitcher Catcher Communication

Leave it to a pitcher that graduated Stanford with a communications degree to expound on pitcher catcher communication.

Jack (Black Jack) McDowell was drafted by the Chicago White Sox in the first round (fifth pick) of the 1987 baseball draft after a stand-out baseball career at Stanford University. After only six games in the minor leagues, he made his Major League debut on 15 September 1987. McDowell then became a three-time All Star, back-to-back 20-game winning, and Cy Young Award winner. He has since impacted the lives of many collegiate ball players, younger, newer professionals as well as up and coming younger players. You bet he knows all about pitcher-catcher communication.

When asked about typical and most common communication between pitchers, catchers, and managers, he got right to the point and spelled it out clearly. As a note, Jack is more of a baseball traditionalist and looks at players and the game of baseball and the mental side of the game, without diving deep into things like analytics. More about that shortly.

Jack bluntly shared that if the manager came out for a mound visit, the pitcher, knew almost instantly that they were gone and out of the game. If a pitching coach made the mound visit, it would evolve into a conversation that could consist of a reminder about scenarios discussed in pre-game plans or specific talk about scouting report information and how to get a particular batter out. A pitching coach might also tell the pitcher about something mechanically observed, that the pitcher was a little off about. Sometimes, viewing from the side of the field, with a coach's viewpoint, is a better perspective to see things that might be off and why a particular pitcher wasn't having the desired command of pitches expected.

Back in the day, before mound visits were limited, there was more catcher-pitcher mound visits. Usually then and certainly during the days before pitchcom, a catcher would talk about a change of the signs, especially when an opposing runner is on second base. That was very normal and typical. Another significant point that led to more communication is that catchers are, as Jack says, "…very available to observe a pitcher's mechanics." Catchers are very adept at that because they catch the pitcher on side days practice; they know what a pitcher is doing or should not be doing that is preventing a pitcher from being able to do what is expected or what he wants to do. The catcher will let a pitcher know what adjustments to make along with other tweaks or suggestions for improved performance.

Jack says emphatically, "That's Baseball. Jack is emphatic and says that "Baseball is pitch to pitch adjustments." There is a lot in that edict, and he emphasizes that now, and when he played. No matter who you are or how good you are, you are never going to produce every single thing on every single pitch as a hitter, pitcher, or defender. That's just the way baseball works."

That 'adjustment,' emphasis is what makes Jack not shy about stating his stance on analytics. He states that analytics 'predetermine,' things that should be left to 'in-game' pitch adjustments, again reiterating his emphasis on pitch-to-pitch adjustments.

He goes on to state, "…there are things that can be done to predetermine but that should go with the practice of being able to read, in a pitcher's mind and with his own baseball knowledge and experience, what actually is happening on the field and how to approach a particular hitter coming up to bat; it's all about knowing the players and understand what's going on, what's going well and what's not going well." Jack states that analytics drive now, when pitchers come in the game and go out of the game. Usually, it should be the other team, along with a pitcher's performance, that would signal the time to take the pitcher out of a game.

McDowell was a no-nonsense, to the point pitcher. Because of that, there was no surprise when asked about his recollection of any funny mound visit conversations. He laughed and was quick to point out that he felt that those types of conversations happened only in the movies. *Baseball Confidential* shares lots of humor in mound visit situations but saved until later chapters.

He never experienced that humor. Mound conversations were mostly specific on the game, the situation and how the pitcher was doing which led to talk of the adjustments the catcher suggested to the pitcher.

Jack continued to emphasize the mental side of pitching and communication, verbal and non-verbal that affected that. Speaking of non-verbal affects, one of Jack's frustrations was when he faced a particular, behind the plate, umpire. One particular umpire he encountered each season, didn't make any physical moves when calling a strike or a ball. Jack, the pitcher didn't know what the result of the pitch was in that situation and that admittedly had a definite mental effect on him. He soon realized what that affect was. If he knew the count on the batter, he could strategically choose or think about his next pitch and mentally prepare accordingly. Instantly, seeing whether a pitch was a strike or a ball and knowing the count would allow that to happen.

Jack is active with giving back and teaching younger players the art of pitching. Coaches call the pitches and game at little league levels, so young pitchers don't really go through the mental preparation to make pitches; a pitcher doesn't get ready to throw until the catcher puts down the signs. Throwing on side days, practicing pitchers know the pitch that is going to be thrown beforehand and can be get ready mentally. In view of this, young pitchers need to practice the mental preparedness required for pitching. They have to think of knowing what to throw and the related mental preparation for the pitch. Once the pitcher gets ready and starts the motion, McDowell suggests, that a pitcher needs to visualize, seeing in their head, what the end result of the pitch will/should be. That will/should be so that it will train the brain to do that every single time the pitcher gets a call from the catcher. This proves to be way better than seeing the catcher's sign and throwing without any mental preparedness.

One scenario of mound visits is the manager walking to the mound with intentions of a pitching change. There have been times where the pitcher works hard and is successful at talking the manager into not replacing him and leaving him in the game. Jack McDowell doesn't remember any situations that he was involved in where this happened, getting back to his no-nonsense traditional approach to pitching.

Thinking about being taken out of games, a review of the stats showed an interesting point. Jack McDowell had 64 no decisions in his career and his era in those no decision game was 2.12; his best games were games where he received no decisions, win, or lose, on the game.

Baseball is about communication. Jack McDowell lived and practiced all those aspects related to this key component of everyday baseball games.

Tom Browning – Personal Catchers

Tom Browning was an All-Star pitcher who threw the only perfect game in Cincinnati Reds history and helped the team win a World Series title. Browning was known not only as a great left-handed pitcher but also as a colorful, different kind of guy, character. He once left the Wrigley Field visitors bullpen and sat in full Cincinnati uniform with Chicago Cub fans atop a rooftop, in plain sight with many fans, across the street during a Reds-Cubs game in July 1993.

Paul Daugherty, a retired newspaper sports columnist and self-proclaimed quasi-expert on all things Cincinnati said about Tom and his Reds teammates, "…they were all Just Guys. They were genuine, they respected the people who worshipped them. They were, generally speaking, 'good people' as former University of Cincinnati basketball coach Bob Huggins liked to say."

Tom Browning was good people. Tom Browning cared nothing about his ego. He signed a lot of autographs, even after he threw the perfect game. I realized this phenomenon firsthand. Tom and I were setting up an interview to talk about *Baseball Confidential* and Tom's book, *Tales from the Cincinnati Reds Dugout.* As we were scheduling and trading availability all of us in, the baseball world got news we didn't want to hear. Tom Browning had died. He was 62 and not a lot of information on his cause of death. This was painful and sorrowful. The whole baseball world was in mourning. It's sad for me to even write this.

Despite never being able to carry out the full interview, I was able to pick up information from his book made available to me to go with the other Tom Browning information.

We talk about catcher trust and how well catchers know pitchers and how they interact with pitchers while being completely in synch. His catcher for his perfect game was Bo Diaz. Diaz played almost every day in the season that Browning threw his perfect game, including another 'almost' no-hitter by Browning earlier that year. Diaz was an All-Star, a player on a National League pennant winning team and a member of the Venezuelan Baseball Hall of Fame. Diaz knew catching. Diaz knew his pitchers. Bo Diaz was Tom Browning's personal catcher.

The concept of personal catchers, the pairing of regular, every day, star pitchers with a preferred backstop for a majority of their starts, has been around for decades. With a personal catcher, a pitcher is more comfortable throwing to a catcher that knows the pitcher and knows how to call the game/pitches that work best for him.

The catcher and pitcher have to be in sync about their pitching plan and their approach with each batter. This has to be reconciled with what the catcher knows is working from a pitcher on a particular day and what is not working. A personal catcher offers a pitcher the opportunity to create a better rapport with them on all these types of game decisions.

When the Chicago Cubs signed pitcher Jon Lester to a multi-year contract, they went shopping and got David Ross. David Ross was Lester's personal catcher for more than one team. There are many other pairings of note that can be classified as personal catchers: Clayton Kershaw wanted personal catcher A.J. Ellis, so the Los Angeles Dodgers resigned him for Kershaw. Johnny Cueto pitched the best when Brayan Pena was catching for him as his personal catcher in Cincinnati. Other personal catchers of note are Tim McCarver for pitcher Steve Carlton in St Louis and Eddie Perez for Greg Maddux in Atlanta.

Sports Illustrated reported in early 2021 that the MLB has seen the continuation of a long-standing trend of personal catchers, just like Tom Browning and Bo Diaz. Beyond that, Tom considered Bo a quiet leader as he commanded respect from all pitchers. In Tom Browning's book, *Tales from the Cincinnati Reds Dugout*, he states about Bo Diaz, "When his pitchers failed, he often took responsibility. When we succeeded though, Bo gave us all the credit."

This concept became very much in play in many catcher-pitcher exchanges during games.

Tom Browning was just a rookie for the Reds. Bo Diaz was catching him in one of his games. Browning tells of many times Diaz would flash pitching signs to Browning and Browning would shake the sign off. He'd flash the signs again and Browning would repeat his dissatisfaction with the signal. I call the catcher-pitcher communication without the mound visit. If Diaz got shook off too many times, he would look at Browning on the mound from his catchers crouch and do nothing but calmly point to his head, a finger almost jabbing the top of his skull. This was the signal to the pitcher, Browning in this case, that Bo probably knew something that the pitcher didn't about the situation, the strategy and mostly about the batter at the plate. Bo knew. Browning trusted his catcher implicitly and went on with his pitching, usually with a successful response. None of that would have existed without the personal catcher relationship developed in this case.

In his book, Browning went on to share another Bo Diaz instance. It was during a season where Browning was challenged with successive starts. Hitters were unloading on him game after game. After about four unsuccessful starts, the Reds' management decided to move Browning to the bullpen. Browning always dreaded that move before, during and after it was made. He ended up making one relief appearance. Through a combination of Browning's ineffectiveness as he states and the umpire's apparent refusal to call strikes, his personal catcher, Diaz just quit flashing pitch signals. He briefly visited the mounds and told Browning to just throw the ball hard and hope for the best. Believe or not, Browning followed that meeting by pitching two scoreless innings. He remained in the bullpen despite any performance as management's plan had already been made.

Fast forward to another Tom Browning pitched game. He recalls his entry, still as part of the dreaded bullpen, being in the seventh inning of a particular game. He was facing the top of the Dodgers lineup for the third time through the batting order. Browning had an epiphany that he referred to as a light bulb moment. His thought was all that he needed to do was to get every opposing batter out just one more time. Browning got excited. He was ready, as he said to mow them down right away.

Manager Pete Rose thought that Browning got into pitching trouble when he got excited and started pitching faster, to try and 'mow down' every hitter coming to the plate. Browning always worked quickly but if he worked too quickly, as his manager knew, he would throw pitches in the prime hitting spot right over the plate. Nothing good usually comes of that.

Jeff Reed, who was a catcher for many Major League teams was Browning's catcher that night. Reed told Browning after the game that manager Pete was worried about Browning's pace and ensuing results. Pete continually signaled to catcher Reed from the dugout, to have Reed tell Browning to slow down. According to Browning, Reed would try to buy time between pitches fiddling with the ball and standing up to stretch his legs between pitches, fiddling with the ball some more and standing up to stretch his legs before he'd return the ball back to Browning. Occasionally, Reed would raise both his hands and just put out some kind of signal for Browning to slow down. Sure, a mound visit would have done the same, but Reed and Browning were mostly always on the same page and Browning knew what his excitement would cause.

It was that night that as Browning says, everything clicked. His pitching was just as he planned. He felt almost invincible. Rose would have said vulnerable. In situations like that, he is quick to admit that 'Only rarely do you feel that type of invincibility on the mound. And when it happens you can't pitch quickly enough.' That explains Browning's pace and Reed's need to continually coach his pitcher to slow down. As we hear of many other mound visits, that often is a popular reason to call time out, visit the pitcher and let him breathe. That slows things down and success is more probable.

David Ross and Jon Lester – Knowing the Pitcher and Refocusing

There is no doubt about the relationship between pitcher Jon Lester and catcher David Ross. Lester announced his retirement and probably is on his way to a berth in Cooperstown with the Baseball Hall of Fame. Ross is the current manager of the Chicago Cubs. Lester and Ross have long been friends. It's been talked about a lot in their recent careers. We've talked about the concept of a personal catcher. Ross was the epitome of that for Lester. Lester, served as his personal catcher with the Red Sox (2013-14) and Cubs (2015-16). The two were on teams together that won two titles (2013, 2016), the latter in Ross' final big-league playing season after he followed Lester to the North Side of Chicago to join the Cubs. This bond between the two has been shaped over five seasons, two teams and 100+ starts.

Lester won his first two World Series championships with the Boston Red Sox. He attributes much of his gritty attitude, character and will to win to catcher David Ross. It is reported that in Boston, and he also learned what being a good teammate on and off the field meant. Ross played a key role in this.

Ross tells of a time in a game, Boston Red Sox against the Oakland As. Lester had struck out twelve batters in seven innings. At the beginning of the eighth inning, Lester walked the leadoff on four pitches that didn't look like they came from Jon Lester's normal quality of pitching.

Ross walked out to the mound and started screaming at Lester, "Are you done? If you're done, I'll let [Red Sox manager John] Farrell know."

Lester fired back, mostly yelling, "We're not done." Ross retreated to his catching position and Lester struck the next three Oakland batters to bring his total to fifteen strikeouts for the day. Was it the mound visit, Lester's fierce attitude and approach or a combination of the two that produced? You be the judge.

Secondly, this next mound meeting story gives an idea what it's like to deal with the aggressive and demanding Lester.

Lester was on the mound. Ross was behind the plate catching. They were at the infamous Fenway Park in Boston, playing the Detroit Tigers. At the time, the Tigers were a powerhouse team. They had a great lineup and sometimes feared, probably not by Lester. Boston had a lead. Reports vary as to whether it was a two or three run lead, but they had the lead.

There was a lot going on in the game, it was late, probably about the sixth or seventh inning and the Red Sox third baseman missed the ball that was hit to him; clearly an error and the ball cruised by him. Lester was livid. Lester always did pitch with a chip on his shoulder, usually in a good way and had the highest of expectations of himself and other players on the team. This error bugged him. He showed it. He walked the next batter. A couple of batters later, Lester had a bases loaded situation. Thankfully, at this time, there were two outs. Miguel Cabrera of the Tigers approached the plate. Cabrera can be an intimidating hitter without Lester thinking about his third baseman's error. With the walks and now bases loaded situation, Lester's body language was obvious to anyone caring to look. Ross later reported that it was bad, speaking of the body language.

I don't have the exact conversation or quotes, but the conversation was more or less a breather for Lester. Ross approached and Lester was still fuming about his teammate's error. In Rossy style, he told him to forget about that previous errant play, focus on the job at hand, get his act together and get an out. Little did he need to remind him that in their situation, they could lose the ball game with one swing of the bat by the opposing batter.

That one mound visit did the trick. Fortunately, no catcher knew his pitcher better than Ross knew Lester. Pitchers think in different ways and many think of many things at the same time. Being as professional and experienced as they are, no one would have expected that a pitcher like Lester would let an error from three plays ago throw him off. Ross knew. Ross knew that he had a job to refocus Lester on the job at hand with one batter at a time. That's the catcher knowing his pitcher which has been discussed repeatedly.

Rossy's encouraging words, while getting into the head of his pitcher, inspired Lester to have a strong finish, as Lester finished the inning very successfully, walking off of the mound joyful and proud. That's just as much a reward for the catcher as it is for the pitcher.

David Aardsma – Middle Inning Focus and Recalibration

Baseball players have lots of stories. They go through many experiences from college to the minor leagues and then the big show. A lot of stories would be expected with these varied paths. What I have found is that pitchers seem to have a lot more instances worth talking about. Some of the stories are serious, some are funny, and many are eventful and memorable. That was certainly the case in talking to former MLB pitcher, David Aardsma.

David Aardsma last pitched in the major leagues in 2015, with Atlanta. His best years were with the Seattle Mariners, where he performed mostly as a closer saving 69 games from 2009-2010. Saves were nice, but most of the time he filled the role of middle inning reliever in his seven club, nine-year MLB history.

Aardsma, who is now the Toronto Blue Jays player development coordinator, is a former first-round MLB draft pick, led the Rice Owls to a College World Series championship in 2003, and took over first place in the all-time major league alphabetical listing, bumping the infamous Hank Aaron. You can bet a player with this track record will have stories.

In talking with David about mound visits with pitchers, he discusses much of what every other pitcher talks about, but he does offer a few twists. Realizing that there are many reasons for mound visits, he still says they can be peculiar. Aside from the peculiarities he said, ninety percent of the time, the same things are talked about with every pitcher on every mound visit. Pitchers can repeat these messages and conversations in their sleep, they hear it so much: "You have good stuff, just throw strikes."

"It's time to get strike one."

"This batter is prone to pulling the ball to left field, all the time."

"Watch the runner on second base." Other situations are discussed but at the end of all this, David will say mound visits are usually made to give the pitcher a break and a breather.

David offered one of the better quotes related to this when he said, "Pitching is about slowing down and hitting is about speeding up." As pitchers (and batters) remember this, they will pace themselves accordingly. If they don't, they have to be reminded to slow down or speed up. For pitchers, this usually results in a mound visit.

David was reluctant to name names for his stories but finally did. Aardsma played his college ball for Rice University. He played for legendary coach, Wayne Graham. After 26 full seasons at the helm of the Rice baseball program, and 37 seasons as a collegiate head coach, Graham is known as one of the top baseball coaches in the country, having built a solid baseball program at Rice.

Graham did play in the major leagues before that for Gene Mauch's Philadelphia Phillies and for legendary Hall of Famer Casey Stengel and the New York Mets.

Aardsma was on the mound, in one of his college games. He was struggling a bit. He normally pitched well and was, at this point of his college career, setting up to be in the top ten of the MLB draft. In fact, this was the year Rice won the national championship. Aardsma talked about a two-week stretch of games where the team did not play at a championship level. He said those two weeks were bad and he was one of the guilty ones contributing to that demise. He was on the mound and not pitching well. In this game, he was about to give up the chance for victory. Manager Graham calls time and walks out to the mound. He was furious. That seems to be characteristic of a lot of managers when a pitcher is underperforming. That was the case here. He told Aardsma point blank, "If I could shoot you in the head and kill you, it would make me feel really good, but I can't do that because it's illegal." Graham turned around and walked back to the dugout, saying no more. Imagine a young kid, hearing that kind of message from someone they looked up to. Graham was extremely frustrated. He knew he couldn't say that message to anyone, but Aardsma, so he did. That was harsh, but Aardsma pitched out of the inning and Rice won that game. Graham's mission of motivation, regardless of style, was accomplished.

Another instance with manager, Wayne Graham came again during a time where Aardsma was again struggling on the mound. He admits to the struggling at that point but was at a point in his career that he was, 'starting to figure it out.'

Graham walked to the mound and told Aardsma, "You've got nothing and I'm going to take you out. Look down at the bullpen. Relief pitcher, Wayne Townsend is ready and warmed up (Townsend saw the mound visit and when Aardsma turned to the bullpen to see what Wayne Graham was referring to, Townsend waved to him)."

Graham went on and asked Aardsma, "Why shouldn't I bring him in?" Aardsma had the perfect reply now that it can be talked about. He told Graham that he had a changeup pitch ready and with the hitter coming up, he could get him out with that pitch. Graham told Aardsma that he would give him one more pitch and then he would bring in reliever Townsend. Here's where full disclosure comes in. Aardsma and the catcher looked at each other after Graham left the mound and the catcher said, "You haven't thrown a change up all year." Aardsma knew that but that was his reply to his irate manager at that point in time. Aardsma proceeded to throw the best changeup pitch that he had ever thrown, and the batter fouled it off.

Here's where the story gets even better. Wayne Graham started out of the dugout on his way to the mound just like he promised after that one pitch. The relief pitcher Townsend was running in from the bullpen to the mound. Before Graham crossed the foul line into the field of play, the umpire stopped him and told him not to go to the pitcher's mound. He could not have two visits in one at-bat, by rule. Graham yelled to Aardsma that this for sure was the last batter he would face and then Aardsma would be replaced. Aardsma stayed in the game and threw another changeup. He struck the batter out and they were out of the inning. Aardsma was so fired up, very emotional, almost in an over-the-top manner and went into the dugout, very boastful and pointed (pointing is never suggested) and told his manager, "I got this."

Aardsma's pitching coach grabbed him, pushed him up against the wall and said, "You never talk to our coach like that." The message was sent and Aardsma calmed down outwardly, even though inside he was still emotional and elated.

After the game, word was sent to Aardsma, that manager Graham wanted to talk to him in his office. The immediate thought that went through Aardsma's head, at that time, was this was his final game ever. That's the message he was expecting from his manager. Fortunately, for David Aardsma, that wasn't the case. Manager Graham said to him, "I love what you did. I love that you yelled. I wanted that emotion out of you and I finally got it. Don't ever do it again. Do it privately. Don't do it in front of the rest of team."

That was an even greater message sent to Aardsma that stuck with him the rest of his career. That coach wanted Aardsma to be a bulldog and that was his way of coaching him to that point.

Understanding mound visits and the communication that goes on during those has revealed many instances, some serious, some belligerent and some very funny. This next incidence is in that last category.

David Aardsma was pitching for the Seattle Mariners at the time. His pitching coach was Rick Adair, and his manager was Don Wakamatsu. Wakamatsu is a former catcher, coach, manager, and scout and liked to be in charge. Aardsma had a good relationship with the bullpen coach, John Wetteland, in addition to the other coaches mentioned. Aardsma called it a perfect storm set up to have a great pitching year and experience. He was in a game in a season where he was having a good year. In the game, he was struggling a bit. He described it as kind of struggling and kind of not. He could be out of an inning with one swing and miss or a pop out of any kind, but he was beating himself. He had two on base and one out. Pitching coach Adair, made a mound visit. It was a one-run game. He was used to being visited in these situations.

Adair approached Aardsma on the mound and all he said was, "Nod." Aardsma, following his coach's directions, nodded. Adair said that was perfect. He said do that again, right now. Aardsma nodded. Adair then admitted that his manager, Wakamatsu wanted Adair to make the mound visit to offer words of wisdom. Adair didn't think he needed to but had to follow his manager's direction. He repeated again and asked Aardsma to nod one more time. He said, "You're killing it. Perfect!" He then started talking about observations of people in the stand, usually the good-looking girls, nothing baseball related. He finished by saying, "Go get 'em."

Aardsma knew that it was mostly about getting his mind off whatever he was doing that wasn't up to par. That mound visit took his mind off the pressure of the game and maybe baseball in general. That was the purpose. Aardsma explains it as a recalibration. A coach can't visit and say, 'recalibrate.' No pitcher would be able to recalibrate with that instruction. Recalibration comes when taking their mind off the situation in total. Aardsma even said one coach told him to look at the flagpole. That's a total distraction and served its purpose.

There were a lot of commonalities with these stories that other pitchers have offered. It further emphasizes that it's a people game. It's a mental game and there are ways to make that better during games for pitchers. David Aardsma is that case in point.

Catchers

Mike Heath – Experienced Catcher

It's exciting and sometimes revealing to hear about the exchanges on the mound. If we had a microphones on each player during those chats it would be even better but for now, we will rely on *Baseball Confidential*. Hearing chats is one thing but seeing a mound visit in action and no chat happening is different.

Mike Heath shares experiences that reflect that.

In 1981, the Oakland A's under manager Billy Martin were playing a mid-summer game. On the mound for Oakland was pitcher, Steve McCatty. Players, managers and even some fans called him, 'Cat,' for obvious reasons.

Mike Heath was McCatty's catcher for that game. Mike was the starting catcher for Billy Martin and his highly successful early-80s Oakland A's teams. Mike Heath was a catcher who came up with the 1978 Yankees and was part of their World Series championship team. He also was a strong influence on a great group of younger pitchers in Oakland.

Steve McCatty happened to be having a very good game. Some would describe his performance as stellar, at least, most observers would. One observer had a slightly different opinion. That observer was manager Billy Martin watching McCatty from his perch in the dugout.

Billy, from his managerial helm signaled and pushed catcher Mike Heath to make a mound visit and go talk to the pitcher. Usually, a mound visit and chat is suggested when there are problems, when adjustments are needed or the pitcher needs a breather. None of those situations existed at the time Billy was pushing for a visit. Catcher Heath was a bit confused but didn't tell his manager. Heath thought to himself, McCatty is 'dealing,' he was getting guys out. His pitchers were being located with good command and he was what most would say, on a roll. Heath could not figure out why Billy Martin pushed for a mound visit but being the good catcher that he was and loyal player, he called time out to make the mound visit that manager Billy wanted him to do. On his way out to the mound, he told me that he was thinking, "What am I going to talk to him about. He's pitching fine. No adjustments are needed, and he doesn't even need a breather or change of pace."

Now here is where it gets interesting and almost comical. Heath gets to the mound, looks at pitcher McCatty and starts moving his mouth like he would if he was talking but didn't say anything. There was no voice, just mouth movement. He did it for more time than you would guess. Pitcher McCatty looked at Heath with a strange gaze and for sure, was thinking, *what is this guy doing*? Cat couldn't figure out, with all his pitching experience, what was going on, what Heath was trying to accomplish with that mound visit. Heath kept 'talking,' and still was just moving his mouth with no voice coming out. Heath finished, 'talking,' gave him a pat for good luck and returned to his position behind the plate. A few pitches later, the A's got out of the inning as Cat retired the side.

After the third out, Cat and the rest of the team retired to the dugout. Cat eagerly sought out his catcher and asked what was wrong with him. He sincerely wanted to know if he was alright. Heath came clean and said manager Billy Martin wanted catcher Heath to have the mound visit and conversation and Heath didn't agree with it. Heath clearly stated that there was nothing constructive that he could say, so he went through the motions of talking, moved his mouth actively, and finished with no damaging words or any words, for that matter. He just wanted Billy Martin to think that his directive was being carried out as he wished. It's unclear whether Heath ever came clean with Martin, but in that case, all missions were accomplished.

I'm not sure why Steve McCatty keeps showing up in mound visit conversation stories, but Mike Heath shared another one.

Being the Cincinnati Reds fan that I have been to many of their games, I still get to experience an age-old Cincinnati tradition. That tradition is when a Cincinnati batter hits a home run, fireworks are fired off outside the stadium in full celebration. Crowds love it and many go to the game for the fireworks. Comiskey Park in Chicago has that same tradition doing the same celebration, with a centerfield fireworks display, for each home run.

According to Heath, Steve McCatty was on the mound this particular night at Comiskey with the Athletics playing the White Sox. He was an emergency starter after planned starting pitcher, Mike Norris couldn't go. Norris came up sick the day of the game. McCatty started the game and was pitching fairly well (up to a point). McCatty gave a home run to the opposing White Sox player and as is tradition, the fireworks were on full display after the hit. The Athletics viewed that as manageable, as that is baseball and expected now and then.

The umpire gave Heath the new replacement game ball which he threw to pitcher McCatty. On the very next pitch, McCatty gave up another home run. Off went the fireworks with the crowd in a frenzy. Fans wanted even more fireworks. At the time, the Athletics had a 4-run lead. With McCatty's served up homeruns, that lead was getting cut into. Managers and pitching coaches viewed giving up a lead as something worse than trying to get a lead. That was not necessarily a good situation for pitcher McCatty.

Art Fowler, pitching coach called time, and strolled to the mound. That stroll could probably be classified as an amble as it was slower than normal. Back-to-back home runs meant back-to-back fireworks, thus Fowler's mound visit. Fowler walked up to McCatty with McCatty stating that he felt fine (indicating his wish to remain in the game), was under control and that he just gave up a couple of mistake pitches. McCatty wanted to wave the coach off and send him back to the bench and make it a short visit and a nice little break in the action.

Fowler looked at McCatty and said, "Cat, I know you're fine. I didn't come out here to talk about your pitches. You're not doing too bad. I'm just killing time so the stadium guys can get the fireworks ready for the next guy. I'm giving the Comiskey firework staff more time to load their cannons." I'm not sure what happened next, but it is just one funny moment between pitching coach and pitcher, that catcher Mike Heath heard standing on the mound with them.

Mound visits and chats with the pitcher aren't always the wisest solution depending on the circumstances. Heath tells of a game in Milwaukee (still with the Oakland A's) against the Brewers with Steve McCatty pitching again, (For the record, Heath did catch for more pitchers than McCatty). It was a tight game. Leading scores were exchanged back and forth. Pitchers in tight games usually garner more attention and focus from managers and the pitching coach. McCatty had his share of focus again. Ben Oglivie was up to bat for the Brewers. *Baseballegg.com* described him, Oglivie as a Stringbean power hitter for the Brewers during the Yount-Molitor years. On deck was Ted Simmons. Simmons, a future hall of famer, hit for a.300 average seven different times in his career and hit 20 home runs six times. He was a power hitter and many times a feared hitter. Pitching Coach Fowler and manager Billy Martin could be seen strategizing in the dugout. Out of the dugout, popped Fowler, on his way to the mound. He wanted to review the strategy he and Billy just talked about, with McCatty and catcher Heath. Fowler said, "Ok, Cat, don't give Oglivie anything good to hit because Billy has the left hander ready in the bullpen warmed up and ready for the batter on deck, Simmons." This was a light bulb moment but not sure whose light bulb it was.

Heath looked at the pitching coach and pointed out that the on-deck batter Simmons that they spoke of was a switch hitter and of late was hitting very, very well against left-handed pitchers. The left-hander replacement pitcher wasn't a solution, and it would probably backfire. Fowler realized the mistake, forgot about the switch-hitting talent, and even said about his good friend and compatriot, "Billy done 'effed' up. I don't know what to do; let me get back to the dugout."

Back to the dugout he went, engaged in more conversation with manager Martin, pointed to switch-hitter Simmons on deck and continued talking. Billy looked over at the batter on deck and as Heath said, looked at us and threw up his hands up, then threw them down almost in disgust and realized he made a mistake in his strategy just then.

McCatty got Oglivie out, stayed in the game and retired the batter Simmons successfully, relieving and exonerating the manager's strategic gaff.

As I mentioned, Heath did catch pitchers other than Steve McCatty. Heath tells of his approach to pitcher Dave Beard one time. Beard seemed like he was being lackadaisical on the mound and in his demeanor. All it took in one mound visit was to for Heath to walk out and tell the pitcher that if he didn't feel good or feel like being there for whatever reason, Heath would tell the manager to bring in the next pitcher. The other option for Beard was to 'choose' in his mindset to finish the game. That brief semi-motivational conversation prompted pitcher Beard to strike out the remaining batters in the inning.

Mike Heath was also a catcher for the Detroit Tigers. During Sparky Anderson's last great run as Tigers manager, Heath was Sparky's catcher of choice. Pitching in a game that Heath was a catcher in, was Jack Morris. Morris, a future hall of famer, went on to appear as a five-time All-Star, and a player on four World Series Championship teams for the Tigers, Twins and Blue Jays. Heath tells of a time where he had to make a mound visit to Morris. Morris clearly did not want to talk. When Heath approached the pitcher's mound, Morris walked off the back of the mound. Heath was all alone at the top of the mound. Heath knew that any conversation would be futile but at least he did offer words to Jack relating to bearing down and expressing confidence that Jack could get the next guy out. Jack was further from the mound when Heath was talking. Heath said he was alone and just talking to himself. Clearly, this was a one-person mound visit. Heath left and Morris continued to pitch. It's not clear how his performance was after that.

Just hearing some of these mound conversation situations is what you get when you talk to someone like Mike Heath who played for Billy Martin, played for the Yankees, was on a World Championship team and was a strong influencer with younger pitchers on all his teams.

Berra-Larsen – Why Catchers Make Great Managers

Much of the premise here is wondering what a catcher says to his pitcher during a mound visit in the heat of a competitive game.

Few positions in sports feel pressure like a pitcher in baseball. Teams, regardless of their talent level can't win if their pitcher can't throw strikes.

Being a pitcher can sometimes be lonely. Standing on the mound, holding a one-run lead, seeing a power hitter next up at-bat can lead to arms feeling very heavy and legs wobbling like a deep freeze shiver. The pitcher is not in command and walks two batters in a row. The pitcher's confidence is almost absent as he sees the next batter approaching the batter's box. That lack of confidence tells that pitcher that the probability of throwing pitches for strikes is nil.

Almost every pitcher we talked to has been in that situation either early in their career or even in later in a seasoned state. Hallelujah for the pitcher. They get their own personal therapist as their playing partner.

That therapist, also known as the catcher, calls time out and makes his way to visit with the pitcher. In a lot of cases, a coach will remain in the dugout but in the days of limited mound visit, that may not always be the case.

The coaches remain in the dugout patiently watching and waiting. The catcher's role, at that take-charge moment, is to reset the pitcher's confidence, mentality and mindset while allowing him to catch his breath, a mental and physical pause. A reset says it all.

No other sport has a personal psychiatrist like player on the field. Keep in mind that the catcher has the same, head-on perspective as a hitter. All other players stare against that grain.

The catcher directs the pitcher and calls every pitch, aligns the defense, and has those key moment chats to encourage, motivate, and coach. The catcher's role as this performance coach can be the difference between a win and a loss.

Sometimes, a mound visit by the catcher, is not the solution.

Take the case of pitcher Don Larsen and Hall of Fame catcher, Yogi Berra.

In 1956, Don Larsen was the spotlight pitcher for the New York Yankees in Game Five of the 1956 World Series against the Brooklyn Dodgers. The Yankees had a nice lead at 2-0. There were two outs. There was a fever pitch roar from the crowd at Yankee Stadium. Why the roar with a 2-0 lead and two outs? Don Larsen was pitching the greatest game in World Series history, a perfect game. The Brooklyn Dodgers sent the minimum number of 26 hitters to the plate, all to no avail. Pitcher Larsen had retired all of them. There had been 23 perfect games in 130 years of MLB history at the time, but no perfect game had ever been thrown in a World Series game. As was reported, Larsen was one out away from immortality.

Years later, Larsen recalled his emotions and talked about going into deep prayer. He thought he was ready to faint at the height of the motion. He wanted to get through just one more out.

Hall of Fame catcher, Yogi Berra, managed the whole game, pitch by pitch. One out remained and he saw Larsen step off the center of the mound. This is always a clear signal of wanting a breather, trying to calm the nerves. In this case, Larsen was trying to do it himself. Most major league catchers would call time, visit the mound, instill a sense of calmness while motivating and encourage the best. Not Yogi. No time out or mound visit from Yogi.

I'm sure Berra was asked about it after the game, but the real report came years later. Berra remembered and was to the point, "I wasn't going out there. Actually, I didn't talk to him the whole game. He sat on one side of the bench, and I sat on the opposite side."

Berra's thoughts and rationale were clear in Berra's mind, if not anyone else's. No one else mattered at that time. Berra was a catcher and in charge of his pitcher.

Berra's said that if Don Larsen was good enough to get 26 consecutive outs without Berra making a mound visit, he was good enough to continue without one and get one more out.

Berra didn't want to break up what he called Larsen's 'flow state,' that was about to put Larsen in the history books. Rather than letting his ego dictate the game, Berra let his knowledge and feel for his pitcher dictate his moves or in this case lack of moves (no mound visit).

Larsen stepped back up on the mound, after calming and resetting himself and promptly struck out the last batter for the only perfect game in World Series history. It was only at that time that Berra made a mound visit. That visit was a visit to jump straight into Don Larsen's arms to celebrate the occasion. That's both a catcher and pitcher's mound visit dream. The lesson here is a mound visit is not always the solution. Also, a good catcher is key, especially when they know their pitcher as well as Berra did.

Rob Leary – Catcher/Manager/Scout

Baseball Confidential is all about gathering and sharing different perspectives among the behind-the-scenes communication that goes on during a baseball game. Most of what we are talking about here and what we wonder about is related to mound conversations. These happen with catcher and pitcher, catcher, pitcher and pitching coach, catcher, pitcher, and manager or just the pitcher and manager. Sure, infielders also sometimes join in as a pact but not as it relates to mound management.

Getting a perspective on mound visit conversations from a scout is a different, valuable look into *Baseball Confidential*, especially from a scout who has also been a player (catcher) and manager.

Rob Leary, known also as a former catcher, is a professional baseball scout and former coach. In 2012, he was bench coach of the Miami Marlins on the staff of the then, new manager Mike Redmond. He had been a coaching assistant with the 2010-2011, Boston Red Sox and an instructor, catcher, and manager in minor league baseball. Currently, he is doing scouting work for the Arizona Diamondbacks. Rob spent 30 of his 36 years in baseball, on the field; the most recent six as a professional scout.

When Rob first started sharing information about mound visit conversations, before he would give actual stories and scripts, he shared a perspective from his viewpoint when watching a game. When he watches a game, he sees major body language going on especially with a pitcher, mannerisms are present and certain game situations arise that influence every play and every player. With his experience and with all those things, he can just about guess what is going to be said during a mound visit, whether by a catcher or coach. *Baseball Confidential* dives headfirst into actual mound conversations while learning from and relating to perspectives, especially from guys like Rob Leary.

Being the catcher that he was, and the position that he knows so well, he professes loudly that catcher relationships are vital to winning. This includes, especially, catcher-pitcher relationships, but also as important, catcher-pitching coach relationships. He takes this thought further by saying that the catcher in baseball has to be an extension of the pitching coach. That alone can dictate a lot of what goes on for mound visit strategies.

Pitching coaches use catchers more than the average fan can see. Catchers can signal to a pitching coach about the state or condition of the pitcher in certain situations. The whole time Rob talked about this, he repeated over and over how vital catcher relationships are. Players and coaches use each other as part of their game management. That sounds ruthless, but that's a fact in baseball strategy.

The baseball strategy or tactic as Rob states it is, "When a pitcher has success, we as catchers and managers of the game, need to see how long that success can be sustained, not only for one game but for every other game in the season. We manage and do all we can to keep that going."

All of this, body language, mannerisms, relationships, game situations, and strategies influence why and when mound visits are made.

As an example, Rob, in his catcher mindset, pointed out that when a pitcher is doing well and has good momentum going in his game, you rarely see a mound visit. Pitchers can talk to catchers and coaches in the dugout between innings. Motivation, adjustments, and mindsets can all be talked about then.

When asked his primary reason for making a mound visit, he stated that most of the time it was to 'settle things' down. Pitchers can start to rush. They let the game speed up. They get into a situation where the rushing makes them 'throwers,' not 'pitchers.'

Rob's intention was to make the mound visit to stop the game. He let the pitcher take a deep breath and many times said that very thing to him. He told him to relax and calm down. There were times when as a catcher, he told the pitcher to forget about the base runners on base. Pitchers always recognize that as a threatened, high-pressure situation. That high pressure needs defused at times. He reminded pitchers at that time that they were in a 'damage control,' situation. *Take a breath and get back to what made you successful.* Pete Rose, used to say, do what got you to the big leagues.

Sometimes, the visit is because of something mechanical noticed with the pitching motion. Rob explains that sometimes a pitcher might be rushing his body and his arm isn't catching up. Rob point blank says, "Slow down." That's pure pitching technique. The catcher stops the action, tells the pitcher to slow his body down and to get the upper and lower half in synch. Believe it or not, just hearing the words, 'slow down,' can calm a pitcher or hearing things like 'getting in synch,' can do wonders for pitching pace and mechanics.

Rob calls it pitching personalities. Once a catcher knows a pitcher, what his repertoire is and what his pitching and game personality is, on and off the field, the catcher then knows how to handle mound visits. Knowing this also will help the catcher determine whether he needs to signal to the pitching coach or manager that its time they make the mound visit. Relationships and knowing the personnel are key behind each and every pitch, game, and victory.

Many of the things that Rob Leary talks about came into play during one of his playing games when he was at LSU. The manager of the LSU team was Skip Bertman, a former catcher himself, who went on to become the athletic director at LSU. Skip is known as the person responsible, as the subtitle of his book, *Everything Matters in Baseball* states, for building the LSU baseball program from scratch to a dynasty with five national championships from 1991-2000. During Rob Leary's time at LSU, under manager Skip, he was part of the 1986 team that went to the college world series.

Bertman was a former catcher himself. He knew the craft. Because of that, he also knew pitching and was considered a great coach. He was very good with setting up pitchers and guiding pitch types. Once he reached a point of confidence in his catcher to manage a game and once, he felt that a catcher had a 'good feel for a game,' he gave them the flexibility to call pitches.

The game at hand here that Rob shares the story about was a game against Florida State University on a Monday night, *ESPN* game. The game was a tight game, with the teams just separated by a run. It was the bottom of the ninth inning. The pitcher that Rob was catching was Barry Manuel, who went on to play professionally for the Texas Rangers in the American League followed by three other National League teams. Manuel was having a good pitching year that year but started, in this game, to struggle with command and control. Keep in mind it was a very tight game. Any interruption of command and control could derail a lead and eventual victory. Manager Bertman knew this, sensed this, and coached with this. All of a sudden at the peak of the loss of command and out-of-control pitching, pitcher Manuel bounced a ball, in front of home plate, to the waiting catcher.

Immediately, manager Bertman got the attention of catcher Leary. He yelled, "Learjet, come over here." Learjet was Rob Leary's nickname in college ball that carried with him through his baseball career. The manager summoned the catcher so he could deliver the message he wanted the catcher to communicate on a mound visit. Manuel's direction was clear. He told Leary to tell the pitcher that on the next pitch, throw the ball as hard as he can throw about. He wanted his best fastball, faster than anything he has ever thrown. Being the good catcher, leader, and follower of directions guy that he was, catcher Leary called time and trotted to the mound to deliver the message. He repeated almost exactly what he was told to communicate. "Rare back and throw your best fastball," Leary exclaimed to the pitcher. There wasn't a lot of imagination needed here. That statement to the pitcher said it all.

Pitcher Manuel, reared back and threw what Leary considered a great fastball. The hitter at the plate for Florida State University was Paul Sorrento, now assistant hitting coach for the Los Angeles Angels ball club. Paul was known as someone who could hit the ball out of the park. Manuel pitched and Sorrento did exactly that. He met the pitch perfectly, squarely at just the right time with just the right impact point with the ball screaming over the right field fence. Leary emphasized that the ball was screaming and jokingly said that the exiting ball went at least twice the speed of the incoming pitch. All Leary said was that's a classic case, and there were more, where a coach's instruction and influenced mound visit didn't work.

Not all mound visits turn out like they are planned. Even catchers make mistakes that cost a pitcher, not to mention the previously mentioned manager's message. Leary is not shy about talking about a time, in the spirit of *Baseball Confidential*, when he clearly made a mistake (or two) that cost his team the game and resulted in one of the firmest, harshest lectures he ever received from a manager.

This was a game in the Florida State League with Leary catching for the minor league team of the Montreal Expos, the West Palm Beach Expos. The pitcher that came in the game as a relief pitcher, was John Marino who played within the Expos minor league system and for the West Palm Beach Expos that day. Marino was short, left-handed with a good curveball that was very effective against left-handed hitters. The game was tied at that point.

Felipe Alou, MLB All-Star, was the manager of the minor league Expos team. Alou was the responsible party for the pitching change and bring Manuel to the mound that day.

Normally, when a new pitcher comes to the mound, it was catcher Leary's standard operating procedure to have their chat and always close it by stating what the first pitch would be; clear communication with no misunderstanding between catcher and pitcher.

Leary forgot that one policy point in this case. It slipped his mind that he didn't talk about what first pitch to throw.

Sure enough, a big left hander was next up to bat. The at-bat started. The big left-handed hitter had quite a presence. Leary, pitcher Marino, manager Alou and probably anyone that was close to the team knew of that good curve ball that Marino was known for. That one pitch got a lot of batters out and proved to be very successful for him. So, with a power hitter up, Leary dropped the signs behind the plate. The sign was obviously for that great curve ball, which was all the buzz. Pitcher Marino waved him off, asking for another pitch. Leary knew the power of that pitch especially against the batter at the plate. He signaled again for the curve ball. The pitcher shook the sign off again. Usually, when that happens, the catcher and pitcher need to get on the same page. Normally they are, especially with Leary's policy of always communicating that first pitch. Leary visited the pitcher and pitcher Marino exclaimed, "I want to throw a fast ball, not a curve." Leary knew that was not the right pitch, but he gave in.

Leary, crouched behind the plate set up for a fast ball. The pitch came and it was a glorious fastball, a nice heater in baseball terms. It couldn't have been more down the middle than it was. You can guess the result. Sorrento smacked a bases loaded three run triple to break the tie score.

After that hit, manager Alou darted out to the mound. He knew what happened. He didn't even look at the pitcher who gave up the pitch. He stared at catcher Leary and was steaming, livid and all those other hot terms for someone when they were stark raving mad. He proceeded, as Leary describes to 'undress' Leary for an inordinate number of times. He was very intimidating. The fans in the stands had to hear the chewing out. It was less than a minute, but Leary said it felt like ten minutes of tongue lashing.

It was Leary's responsibility to the call the pitch. Everyone knew that the pitch should be a curve ball. Leary relented and broke his own rule of not communicating what that first pitch should be. It was in the minor leagues, so Leary viewed it as a learning experience. Not sure if Alou viewed it the same way. Leary institutes his rule of communication because, as he says, "You can't always assume that the pitcher is on the same page as you or the manager."

Leary continued viewing times like this as lessons. Even in his managerial work and working with younger, developing players, he talks about life lessons and learning experiences. He states that in a tight game where it is paramount to stick to a plan and have ideas and communication thought out. The goal is to stop anything from disrupting that before it manifests itself into a three-run triple or grand slam to break the tie and lose the game. Much of baseball takes the shape of life lessons.

James McCann/Brad Ausmus – More About Catcher-Pitcher Relationships

James McCann, now catching for the New York Mets, used to catch for the Detroit Tigers. He is a former All Star, played for the United States national baseball team in the 2011 Baseball World Cup and has caught no-hitters. One of his favorite pitchers was Justin Verlander. Justin, just like many other pitchers, at times shakes off the signal from the catcher. He doesn't like the call and wants to throw a different pitch. That happens often. That's baseball. Sometimes, all that shaking off will lead to a mound visit, so that the pitcher and catcher can communicate. Granted, with the new rules limiting mound visits, this doesn't happen as often, but it still happens.

Many watch the shake offs and ensuing mound visits and conversations and immediately jump to the conclusion that catcher and pitcher are not on the same page. That is sometimes the case but not usually. If there is a runner on second base, the catcher and pitcher may switch their signs. Chris McCosky, writer for *The Detroit News* interviewed and reported on his conversation about mound visits and pitcher/catcher relationships with catcher, James McCann. McCann told McCosky that sometimes he will say to his pitchers, "Hey, this is what our game plan is, bud, do you think we should stick with it here?" Or other times, "I know we said no changeups here, no changeups or sliders to this guy, but I think we can throw one here. What do you think?"

Believe it or not, that's typical of mound visit conversations. It depends on the pitcher-catcher relationship and what they talk about before the game. Every pitcher-catcher has a game plan that is discussed. The perfect scenario is that the game goes according to the plan, but most times, adjustments need to be made.

McCann further told McCosky, "For the most part, it's just talking something through. I know a lot of people think, 'Oh you've got to make a mound visit, obviously you aren't on the same page'." McCann went on to say, "The reality is, it's more to make sure you talk something through." Being on the same page is different than that. "You may not be 100 percent on something, or you don't want to just have the pitcher shake off signal after signal."

Sometimes, the pitcher is right and emphatic and sometimes, the catcher is most sure.

McCoskey shares again in his *Seattle Times* article, McCann described another start where a situation called for a fastball. That was the signal he, the catcher, gave to the pitcher. The pitcher shook off the signal. McCann gave the same signal and was again called off. That prompted a request for a time-out and a trot to the mound for the proverbial catcher-pitcher conversation. The exchange goes something like this: The pitcher says, "Hey, I don't want to get beat with the change-up here."

Catcher McCann pushes back and says, "I don't want to get beat with a slider." McCann expected from the pitcher, a statement of agreement or a strong case, plea, and directive to throw the slider anyway.

McCann told the pitcher that if he did throw the slider here, "Make it a good one." That particular rhetoric is common in mound visit communication. Catchers, many times, do say, after the pitch type is decided upon, to make a good pitch. That's the conversation.

McCoskey wrote about a few other pitcher-catcher exchanges that resemble much of the same feedback I heard during interviews with players and coaches. McCoskey also reports that Manager Brad Ausmus caught 18 seasons in the big leagues.

The reasons make great baseball managers when their career end is somewhat obvious. They not only have the whole game in front of them, viewing the entire baseball diamond from their position. They handle the pitching staff and play captain of on field duties among knowing the intricacies and strategies of the game. The catching position prepares them to make the same the manager makes when managing ball games. In fact, fifty percent of the past 20 World Series-winners have been led by managers who were former catchers. So, back to Ausmus.

Brad will tell you that he, much like every other catcher, has had his share of signs waved off by pitchers. He has had mound conversations where his position and opinions were ignored by some of the best pitchers.

Ausmus was honest with the description of his conversations. He indicated he never told a pitcher that he had to throw a particular pitch. Many times, he would take a managerial approach and ask the pitcher what he wanted to throw in a particular circumstance. Ausmus would not hold back, though, of stating his reasons and positions for his preferred approach. Here again if the pitcher chose his way, Ausmus would offer, "Make it a good one." This was sometimes tough because Ausmus knew deep down that the wrong pitch would get blasted for dire consequences (home run). Honestly, Ausmus did say the pitcher would be right.

In the days before mound visit limitations, Ausmus would get blamed for having too many mound visits with pitcher, Roger Clemens, when they played together. Ausmus wanted to be on the proverbial same page regardless of the number of mound visits. Ausmus, took this into consideration and told catcher James McCann, when they were Detroit Tigers together, "If there is any doubt, go talk to the pitcher. I don't care if they yell at you about going out. I would rather you be on the same page than have something screwed up because of miscommunication." That was again, before the days of mound visit limitations.

All of this communication, all of this being on the same page, all of these mound visits are a function of trust built between pitcher and catcher. All of those involved in these conversations will talk about how trust is hard to build up yet easy to break. That's the case in baseball and life. A good manager, catcher and pitcher will work hard to build trust and develop the right relationships.

Pitching Coach

Josh Miller – Serious and Calm Pitching Coach

By now, any avid baseball fan knows that the Houston Astros was awarded the Commissioner's Trophy for winning the 2022 MLB World Series.

They had just enough offense for the six-game series against the Philadelphia Phillies who entered the series after being the No. 6 (last) seeded team in the six-team playoff scenario. A major contributor to Houston's success was their team's pitching. Their staff was classified as having the deepest, most diverse, most dominant pitchers in Major League Baseball in 2022.

Josh Miller had a gradual rise through baseball and the Astros organization to his position of pitching coach to guide that 2022 staff of pitchers. His approach is a bit different as we will see.

Asking him about the success of his newly dominant staff and the secret to building and cultivating such a successful staff, especially in the postseason, Chelsea Janes of The Washington Post reported a statement by Miller:

"It's mostly common sense. Get nasty pitches and throw them a lot."

Janes went on to report that as Miller would explain it, the Astros have plenty of nasty pitches. When looking at spin, the Astros pitchers averaged more spin than any major league team in baseball in 2022. Pitchers throwing four-seam fastballs are an indication that they have a high degree of trust in their pitches. This Astros club ranked in the top three for throwing four-seam fastballs. In addition, they were in the top two for allowing the fewest home runs hit by the opposition.

Josh Miller's new role brought what some termed as a newfound seriousness. His approach was different in coaching in preparation for games and in in-game situations. Some have even termed it a low-key approach.

He also showed how catchers can be relied upon to manage pitchers. Miller also did well to develop the catchers leadership position in relation to staff success. Veteran catcher Martin Maldonado helped the Astros pitching staff translate those nasty pitches into game planning.

Because of his reliance on catchers managing pitchers, Josh Miller was careful choosing when he made a mound visit to visit with a pitcher. He has groomed Astros catchers to gain his utmost trust and pitcher's trust and now encourages catchers to conduct most discussions during games. Miller does watch every move from the dugout and stands by to be ready when the situation calls for him. Catchers have a way to signal to him to join them on the mound. Usually, this is a situation to review or confirm a scouting report on an upcoming batter or to help settle any debate between catcher and pitcher and their viewpoints.

Miller has a relaxed manner and is usually calm, talking in a soft tone that some say it sounds almost like a whisper.

His objective, much like many other pitching coaches, is to bring Houston's pitchers back to the present and put aside the distractions of whatever went awry before the mound visit. Miller's mound visits aren't lectures; they're listening exercises. He arrives with a plan of attack for the opposing batter, or a particular pitch sequence based on scouting reports but reserves a final ruling for the pitcher as collaborative. Comfort is crucial when chaos looms. Miller wants that comfort for his pitchers.

"The ability to listen and react on the fly as opposed to shutting things down – that's the sign of a good coach," reliever Ryne Stanek said, as reported by Janes. "To go out and have an open dialog in those meetings eases tension in those situations. It's a little bit of 'Take a breath. What do you like? What do you feel? What do you see? All right, then make a decision. This is the decision. Go execute.' More often than not, the Astros do execute as they have shown on their way to the 2022 World Series Championship. Josh Miller was asked directly about his mound conversations and player communication by The Matt Thomas show on Houston radio, *SportsTalk 790* who offers in-depth analysis on Houston sports. Here is summary of that interview available from the radio station, *SportsTalk 970*.

Josh was asked about talking with players mid-game. His process consists of reviewing information from the MLB issued, iPads, and that is now common with all teams.

The iPads give him and the pitchers, feedback on things that might not be going according to plan for a pitcher or things related to their pitch delivery going awry. In particular, he talks about pitch velocity or what he calls pitch shapes and pitch usage when attacking a hitter. That's mid-game banter.

Turning to conversation during a mound visit, he started by stating that most of the time, his visit is for the purpose of giving the pitcher a break, asking him to take a breath and focus on the hitter at the plate or the next hitter up.

Matt challenged Josh to talk to him as if he was on the mound in a tense situation and asked him to tell him what the conversation would be like.

Josh gave it to Matt as if he was the pitcher on the mound during his visit. Josh stated that usually he will say, "I'm out here to give you a break, so let's go ahead and focus on the hitter at the plate. We are one pitch away from getting through this. So, let's hold up for this inning." Josh will go on and say, "It's probably it for you, so let's bear down, focus and go over the attack plan for the guy at the plate." As in all conversations, Josh is quick to make sure the catcher is on the same page with the pitcher and then continue with a good plan. As you can see the conversation is deliberate, to the point and no-nonsense all in a nice manner.

Matt asked pitching coach Josh if he was always that polite. Josh replied that he was. He did admit that there are times when he has raised his voice in the heat of passion, but he viewed his role to be a calming influence and presence on mound visits. Josh admitted that usually when he has to make a mound visit, things are not going well with the pitcher. Face to face with the pitcher at that point leads to blank looks back from the pitcher and a quiet demeanor from them. Josh further knows that his job at that point is encouragement.

He also admitted that in the minor leagues there might have been times where he would offer words to help a pitcher lock in and focus that might not be considered as polite and calming. His message always centers around focusing on the present and focusing on the next pitch. Every visit is different depending on the situation and in the minor league a developmental posture is present vs. just winning the inning or game.

Matt's interview really framed up the job Josh is doing in Houston and their results prove that he is approaching the job right.

Admittedly, Josh's new role did bring some newfound seriousness. Strolling to the mound with a game in the balance brings intensity, not present elsewhere. Miller minimizes the intensity, one calming word at a time.

Carl Willis – Pitcher/Pitching Coach

In researching for *Baseball Confidential*, finding premiere coaches and pitchers is what was sought. Finding both in the same person is a bonus. Find both in the same person and that person being a pitching coach is a *Baseball Confidential* bonus.

Carl Willis is a former pitcher in Major League Baseball and at the time of this writing, the pitching coach for the Cleveland Guardians. Coming to Cleveland after spending the 2015-2017 seasons in Boston, he soon realized that

Cleveland had one of the top performing staffs in all of baseball. His impact was felt immediately despite that.

He didn't jump right into analytics only as he has shown the ability to blend old-school pitching and fundamentals with more modern-day applications that round out the essentials of the pitching craft. There is no arguing this as five different major league pitchers have been awarded the Cy Young Award under his teaching, guidance, and coaching.

We will get into his analytical approach and his ensuing communication with pitchers later.

Carl Willis, in his coaching, emphasizes things like centered around principal. Carl calls it conviction.

In a conversation he had with David Laurila of *FanGraphs*, a blog site of everything baseball (www.fangraphs.com), Carl Willis gave an example of that conviction, true *Baseball Confidential*.

Willis conveyed to David Laurila:

"We were in Cincinnati this year, and Brad Hand came in to close the game. There was a bases-loaded situation. There were two outs and he'd walked the previous hitter. Curt Casali came in to pinch-hit. I looked at my notes, and Hand had never faced him. My gut tells me that I need to go out to talk to Brad about how we need to attack Curt Casali in that situation. My baseball instincts told me that this guy is an elite pitcher."

Willis went on to say, "I wanted him to make each pitch with 100% conviction. If I go out and say, 'Hey, your slider needs to be back-door; pitch him down and away,' at some point in the at-bat, that may impact his level of conviction with what he wants to throw. Closers, in particular, are guys you have to really trust. You have to trust what they do to handle those situations. I chose to not make the trip, and Casali flew out."

Will went on to say that if he noticed a flaw in the pitcher's pitching delivery, he would have made a trip to the mound. Sometimes, pitchers are too quick, or they are out of balance and a trip and conversation is necessary to try and right whatever is wrong. If there are no adjustments needed, pitching with conviction wins out. Willis would not make the mound visit for fear of disrupting that 'conviction,' that he coaches hard about.

Earlier, it was mentioned that Willis does blend old tried and true fundamentals with more modern-day applications that round out the essentials of the pitching craft. This translates into a good understanding and use of analytics that is all the buzz of major league baseball today.

Willis classifies it as tracking date in real time, then using and communicating the information.

This is important because we are talking about behind-the-scenes communication and the things that we as fans don't get close to. Now, we are with *Baseball Confidential*.

Willis talks about the use of what is known as TrackMan in baseball. According to trackman.com/baseball, TrackMan Baseball is a 3D Doppler radar system that precisely measures the location, trajectory, and spin rate of hit and pitched baseballs. When using TrackMan in player development, on-field performance is quantified instead of the traditional qualitative assessment.

Why is this important? You will see how it relates to mound visits here.

There are times during a game where Carl would go to the coach managing TrackMan and ask what that coach was seeing. He doesn't monitor it on every pitch but will check in from time to time to see what might show up. In the meantime, if something shows up indicating something was off base, word would get to Cliff quickly.

In that case, Willis states as Laurila reported, "I won't necessarily go to the mound tell the pitcher, 'The spin axis on your slider today is more lateral, so it's flatter.' It's most likely going to be something like, 'Hey, let's use this pitch here.' Then I might have the conversation with him in the dugout between innings. I'll tell him, 'Your slot is a little lower,' or 'You're getting your hand a little too far away from your head today.' Or maybe it's, 'You're sinking into your back leg a little bit more today, which is bringing everything down and causing the ball to be a little flatter',", all in an attempt to get to the issue at hand, in the moment.

That is very productive mound conversation and that's why Carl Willis as many Cy Young award winners (four of them) resulting from his coaching.

We have mentioned pre-game pitching plans. On more rudimentary basis, Carl will state that "A game plan is built upon the presumption that your starter is going to bring his normal game to the table. Some days that doesn't happen. Some days, there is a pitch that's a little off, so an in-game adjustment needs to be made. It might be, 'you can't do X today, and we're in that count.' Ok, how are we are going to compensate? Maybe we need to go with a changeup instead."

Carl is big on having a plan knowing that there will be in-game adjustments to that plan much like we have talked throughout all our mound conversation discussions.

Laurila shared that Carl Willis rounds out his communication and messaging with the notion that, "… hitting is probably the hardest thing to do in professional sports, it's still not easy for pitchers to get good hitters off balance. Pitching is an art. It's something that needs to be finely tuned. It doesn't happen by happenstance nor by having one elite pitch. You have to learn how to pitch. In today's game, we have more tools to make that happen."

Carl Willis – The Art of The Mound Visit

It's worth more to look at Carl Willis and how he relates to *Baseball Confidential* and mound visits.

Joe Noga of *Cleveland.com*, the premier news and information website in the state of Ohio, reported on Carl's mastery in an article appropriately titled, *How Guardians pitching coach Carl Willis mastered the 'art of the mound visit.'* In the whole book of *Baseball Confidential*, many of the stories, strategies, and tactics of mound visits could be classified as an art. Many pitching coaches and catchers feel this is the case. Pitchers might or might not feel the same way.

In Joe's article, he reports that Guardians manager, Terry Francona says there's a certain art behind a pitching coach making a mound visits during a game. If it's an art, then Carl Willis is the master of that art. Francona went further to say, "I don't think its coincidence that when he leaves that mound, a lot of times, things go right." That's exactly the situation every coach, manager, and player wants to be in more times than not.

Willis, in his 19 seasons as a pitching coach has cultivated a reputation among players and coaches for his 'expert feel,' and knowing when a quick trip to the mound can reset the situation for rookies and veteran pitchers alike according to Noga's report.

Manager Terry Francona continued, "He can relate like nobody's business…" referring to Willis.

Players recognize Willis' expertise and feel that it has a calming influence. That's many a times one of the ultimate goals of a mound visit. He is credited for having in-game strategies that pay off for pitchers of all types and levels of experience.

The starting pitchers on Willis' team know and say that Willis has a skill of determining the exact right moment to make a mound visit. When to make a visit is many times, as important as what to say during that visit. Guardians' All-Star pitcher, Shane Bieber states that, "Willis can shift the momentum of a game when he steps out of the Guardians dugout." Calming influences, shifting momentum, suggesting adjustments are all part of a pitching coach's repertoire for mound visits and part of Willis' 'art.' Bieber will further tell that "Carl's got really good feel that goes way beyond mound visits. It's really hard to quantify, but it seems like every time he visits, there's a big ground ball double play or a strikeout or a pop out and the dugout goes crazy. It's a big momentum shift."

With all of that, Bieber will still compliment the advice given by Willis. "He does give good advice. Whether that's stay back or stay closed with your front side or whatever it may be. It may be, hey, you're getting a little antsy here, slow down. And then he'll refresh you on the scouting report for the next hitter coming up."

Bieber does state his thought semi-profoundly, "Nobody wants him coming out there when they're pitching, but everybody wants him coming out there, if that makes sense."

We have heard it from many catchers that the game dictates when the game necessitates a mound visit. It's different from situation to situation and player to player. Guardians' catcher, Luke Maile agrees with this and says that Willis' simplicity leads to success. Pitchers like simple too. Maile has a good way to describe that. He says, "He's never telling you anything earth-shattering. He's just reminding the pitcher of what makes him good and reminding him what the best plan of attack is. He's seen enough baseball to understand when the right time is."

Carl Willis talks about how tense pitching situations can get in a game. He says there are times where he has made a mound visit, cracked a joke, just to lighten mood to ease the intensity of the moment.

A lot of mound visit conversation revolves around giving pitchers a breather at an intense moment of a game. Triston McKenzie of the Guardians says that "Carl never wants the game to speed up on us. He details what the plan of attack is for the hitter just so that you're not up there struggling trying to worry about runners or holding guys on, or how you're going to execute this pitch or that pitch. He just goes out there and tries to simplify the game for you." There's that reference to simplification again. McKenzie is quick to say, Willis is not the type to try and over-coach or get in a pitcher's face about mechanics.

He does, however, gauge a pitcher's 'feel.' Willis used to make multiple trips to ensure pitchers, catchers, and players were all on the same page, but he did say that over time, he felt it more imperative to let preparation, instincts, and experience take over, whether it was a young pitcher or veteran on the mound. Willis attributes that to not breaking the rhythm. He is one not to over coach what has already been prepared, worked on, and planned. That could almost be termed, just staying out of the way; however, there are times when he needs to get in the way. Usually, that is a case when a pitcher needs to slow down. Willis is proud to bring a sense of calm and most of all, to let his pitcher know that things are still ok, he's still in a good position and just to go forward with the game plan.

It's been said before, but Willis makes it a point to talk about a mound visit being a chance for a pitcher to catch their breath, slowdown and as he emphasizes, get a reset. He likes to remind pitchers of the pre-planned game plan or the delivery approach that was worked on, all in an effort to get the pitcher back to what they know and are comfortable with.

Speaking of not getting in the way, Willis relies a lot, like many other pitching coaches, on the catcher. He admits that many times, a catcher's message can do more good than a pitching coach's message.

Players call Willis' visits and mound strategies, 'a master at work.' You can't argue with success. That's why five different major league pitchers have been awarded the Cy Young Award under his teaching, guidance, and coaching.

Umpires

Al Clark – Experienced Umpire

We're hearing about conversations with pitchers, catchers, coaches, and managers. There is one more person on the field that hears players talking – the umpire.

Author Bruce Weber penned the book, *As They See 'Em,* that is an insider fan's account that draws on the experiences of dozens of professional umpires. The book is described as a no-holds-barred insider examination of the private world of baseball umpires, both minor and major leagues.

Author Weber opens the book with:

Millions of American baseball fans know, with absolute certainty, that Umpires are simply overpaid galoots who are doing an easy job badly. Millions of American baseball fans are wrong.

Baseball Confidential agrees with Bruce Weber.

Nowhere in Weber's book does he talk about what umpires might hear in player communication and most importantly, during mound visits. Umpires do hear player talk.

Al Clark, according to Wikipedia and my personal conversations with Al, is a former professional baseball umpire who worked in both leagues from 1976 to 2001. In his 26-year career, he umpired thousands of games, including two World Series, two All-Star Games, and numerous American League Championship and Division series. He's more than qualified to be on the field overhearing or hearing directly, player conversations, including mound visit conversations.

Al shared what he deemed as one of most in-depth conversations he heard in his years of arbitrating and field presence: Short, sweet and to the point.

The particular conversation, that Al refers to, happened back in the day during Billy Martin's short time of managing the Oakland As. Many will remember Billy's aggressive style of play known as 'Billyball' during that time.

Billy's pitching coach (and evening drinking buddy according to Al) was Art Fowler, who went all the way back to the time of the New York Giants. On the mound, on that day, was pitcher Steve McCatty. Although McCatty never blamed Billy, Billy was accused of overusing pitchers and running up high pitch counts which probably had an effect on pitcher's eventual longevity and careers. (McCatty went on to work in radio and TV for the Oakland A's and with ESPN Major League Baseball followed by coaching at the minor and major league level).

Clark was umpiring at the second base position. He remembers it was the second inning of the day game in Oakland. Pitcher McCatty was giving up hits one after another, almost like he was throwing batting practice for the opposing team. Pitching Coach Fowler asked for time out, was granted it and strolled to the pitcher's mound for a conference. Anyone watching this game would realize that with the non-productive pitching going on and the pitching coach making a mound visit, there was bound to be one interesting conversation. According to Umpire Clark, there was. Clark drifted toward the mound. Call it eavesdropping but he was part of the game and right in the middle of the field of play. He wanted to hear this classic exchange. Fowler arrived on the mound and pitcher McCatty did not say anything. Fowler's first words were, "Cat (McCatty's nickname), I don't know what the ____ you are doing but Billy sure is pissed." McCatty looked him in the eye and Coach Fowler turned around and walked off the mound. That's all. No more conversation. The reply that McCatty was trying to come up with was not needed. Clark chuckled under his breath upon hearing that prolific exchange. No one saw that laugh. Clark expected no less from the coach, to be honest.

While this is a short story, it is an underlining foundation of what umpires know about what goes on with players, coaches, communication, and team play. Clark could have predicted that line by Fowler.

Who is closer to pitchers, catchers, and hitters? Umpires are. They see eyes, body language, and actions. Clark will even take this to the next step and talk about how umpires sometimes have to be amateur psychologists. They see the play and know how players respond in certain situations. Umpires can, most times, watch a player's body language and tell whether he will be successful or how he will respond to coaching communication. Umpires can do this many times better than those in the game-players, coaches, or managers. Pitcher McCatty got out of the inning, less scathed, and didn't pitch anymore in that game. He probably wondered to himself, *what kind of pep talk did I just get?*

In 26 years of MLB umpiring, Umpire Clark, standing nearby, used body language every day in handling situations on the field, during arguments, breaking up mound visits or when letting a guy vent and have his say. In all those situations, being the psychologist kicks in.

Umpires can see or sense the tension on a pitcher just by looking at his glare, hitter's reaction to pitches as they grip the bat harder or a catcher holding a caught position to show the umpire something. Umpires are more than arbitrators and that comes in handy in dealing with all communication whether they are eavesdropping on a mound visit conversation or calling balls and strikes behind the plate.

He did have times where he had to break up mound visits. He measured the personalities and viewed the body language and figured out his approach and what he would say. Being around the league for a long-time garners respect from players and coaches in those situations, so that helps craft any communication and response to any pushback. This includes casual comments from players or coaches about how strikes and balls are called by umpires. A pitcher might say I'm not seeing those pitches the same as you are calling. We need those pitches. Al's typical response is you are the one that has to make the adjustment, not me. I'm sure that response is useful and has been used in many umpire/player/coach communication.

Umpire Clark goes on to say that so much of a team's actions and behavior are a function of the personality of the manager. See Art Fowler and Billy Martin, probably two peas in a pod. What is said on the field has a lot to do with how a manager sets up his clubhouse and how he communicates with his players, before a game, after a game or during a game. Anyone that knows Billy Martin can just as easily hear him say the same thing that his pitching coach, Art Fowler said. Every situation is different, and every personality is different. Clark says thank goodness; umpires can be amateur psychologists. What works with Rob Thompson in Philadelphia wouldn't have worked with manager Tony LaRussa in Chicago (when he was the manager). These are two different managers that handle their club differently. This translates to every situation and ensuing communication being different.

All of this is best captured by something that by former baseball executive, and pioneer baseball man, Branch Rickey:

Where do you find such a man: A man involved in a game who has the authority of a sea captain, the discretion of a judge, the strength of an athlete, the eye of a hunger, the courage of a soldier, the patience of a saint and the stoicism to withstand the abuse of the grandstand, the tension of an extra-inning game, the invective of a player and pain of a foul tip in the throat? He must be a tough character, with endurance and the ability to keep his temper and self-control, he must be unimpeachably honest, courteous, impartial, and firm, and he must compel respect from everyone!

Al Clark was a true reflection of what Branch Rickey spoke about. Here, he has offered the inside of umpire's mindset and the resulting activity on the field. Billy Martin and Art Fowler's approach and communication substantiated this. Umpires hear most and know most. Billy Martin didn't want a pitcher that made him mad.

Dale Scott – Another Set of Ears

Hearing more from other MLB umpires continues with the perspective that they too, are another set of ears to hear *Baseball Confidential.*

Umpire Dale Scott spent more than three decades in Major League Baseball umpiring from 1985 to 2017. Dale states that his job was enforcing on-field baseball rules fundamental to the game and making judgment decisions on the activity of the game. When researching the games he umpired, it was apparent that he worked exactly one thousand games behind the plate calling balls and strikes. Dale performed on some of baseball's grandest stages. He called three World Series, three All-Star Games and over 90 postseason games during his career. In addition, he has worked in every MLB stadium that existed during his career, interacted with many club managers and thousands of players. To say that he was a set of ears to hear a lot of player/coach/manager communication would be an understatement.

Scott is known for many things, but umpires always are associated with ejections. One of Dale Scott's more memorable ejects was in 1988 when he ejected Billy Martin. Billy was so hot at that, that he ended up throwing dirt at umpire Scott. That earned him no respect and a three-game suspension from the league. Scott also umpired his share of notable games involving no-hitters and had his share of run-ins with some of the more noteworthy baseball managers during his time. He became a crew chief in 2001 as one of the league's top umpires as he was known as being consistent, reasonable, and approachable.

Asked about conversations around pitcher's mounds that he has overheard or been a part of and he had plenty to share. He indicated that most people would be surprised and probably find funny, what is heard. Sometimes, the obvious is happening: a coach 'chewing butt,' with a pitcher about his performance or lack of. Other times, you will hear a garden variety of pep talks or maybe advice and coaching on how to pitch a particular upcoming batter and really the list goes on from there.

One incident that Scott classified as humorous was a time when Buck Showalter visited the mound.

Buck is a very experienced manager and has made literally thousands of mound visits and is no slouch when it comes to communication. Buck Showalter is a two-time American League Manager of the Year. There are many stories of his interaction (some prefer the term run ins) with umpires. Buck is a former minor league player who never made it to the majors, known for a strong will and an obsession with fundamentals, details, and preparation. You can bet he was more than prepared for any mound conversation or interaction with an umpire that was to happen.

In this instance, Showalter visited the pitcher's mound and started talking to Umpire Scott, not his pitcher. Managers sometimes do this for two reasons. One is to give a firm message about the way the manager is viewing the game and the decisions the umpire is making (mostly in disagreement). The other reason is to stall for time in order to give a warming up bullpen pitcher more time to get ready to come into the game.

On this visit, Showalter started talking to Dale Scott and said, "Dale, I don't know what to do here. I could bring a right hander and that would make sense. This guy really pitches well to the next batter but I'm not sure. I'm really in a predicament here. What do you think?" Umpire Dale immediately knew what was going on there. Buck Showalter was stalling and doing whatever he could to extend the time for his bullpen pitcher to get extra warm up time in. Pitchers, whether starters or relievers, need to warm up their body to get ready to pitch. The old adage when thinking about warming up is pitchers should warm up the body to pitch, not pitch to warm up. That's why Buck wanted more time for his pitcher in the bullpen. That's why Showalter feigned the conversation with Umpire Scott.

Umpire Scott had a classic, rote for umpires, response to Showalter. Scott replied, "Buck, let's be clear about one thing. The reason I am an umpire is because I couldn't play the game. I was terrible at throwing, catching, and batting. My opinion here would surely be catastrophic, so, Buck, you are going to have to do this on your own."

Scott went on to finish, "Here is one thing I can tell you: I have to know your decision right now. (The umpire is charged with keeping the game moving). We need to go.

What is it?" Showalter indicated that the umpire was no help to him in this situation, so he would go with the right hander in the bullpen. Buck was stalling using a little bit of humor. Good for him but good for Scott for keeping the game moving.

Managers do make mound visits for many reasons. One of those reasons is not to talk to the pitcher but to talk to the umpire. The manager knows at one point the umpire will come out to the mound to break up any conference, for the sake of time and keeping the game going. Once the umpire visits, the manager lays into him about questionable calls on certain pitches. Balls and strikes are not supposed to be discussed. We all know they are talked about and sometimes, there are consequences for managers that do.

This was the case in Dale Scott's first ejection of a big-league manager. He recalls that it was the Toronto Blue Jays playing the Detroit Tigers. Hall of Fame manager, Sparky Anderson was the manager of the Tigers. Sparky was no slouch. He is considered to be one of the great baseball men of all time in terms of success, integrity, and personality. Sparky Anderson led the Cincinnati Reds to back-to-back championships in 1975 and 1976. He led the Detroit Tigers to a World Series title in 1984, becoming the first manager to win the World Series in both leagues.

Sparky was a senior, experienced manager. Senior managers liked to work on rookie umpires. That was the case here. Sparky was not happy with Scott's pitch calling behind the plate. He thought Scott's strike zone was skewed. Sparky and fellow coaches and probably a few players had been 'chirping' from the dugout. Chirping consists of slants or yells to get in the head of those that hear the chirps. Usually, chirps are condescending and defensive. Scott heard his share of chirping from Sparky and company. Sparky called time and walked to the pitcher's mound. Usually, the umpire will wait for the conversation between manager and player to start and then go out to hasten them along. Sparky got to the mound and just stood there in total silence. He didn't say a word. He wasn't even talking to his pitcher. Scott knew what was happening. He had seen it before. Sparky was waiting for the umpire visit, so he could have a word with him. Sparky asked Scott upon his arrival, "Where was that last pitch?"

Dale Scott, replied with, "Sparky, we are not going to talk about pitches and strike zones." Sparky emphatically fed back, "The F____ we aren't." (Insert F Bomb here.) At that point, Sparky was ejected from the game. His final words of tirade to Scott included a spraying of chewing tobacco juice all over Scott. It happens in baseball, and it happened to Dale Scott on that day.

Dan Holmes, in a 2016 article for the website, vintagedetroit.com said this about Sparky, "When you manage a long time, you're bound to get tossed from a few games. Sparky, known throughout the league was not tossed out of that many games, comparatively speaking. Overall, Sparky was ejected from 48 games in his total managerial career. (The math suggests this to be fewer than two per season.) So, about every three months, you could expect to see Sparky hit the showers early."

A few years later, Scott had the same situation happen to him in Toronto. The Toronto ball club was being managed by Cito Gaston at the time. Cito Gaston spent more than forty years in professional baseball as a player, coach, and manager. Best known for leading the Toronto Blue Jays to back-to-back World Series triumphs in 1992 and 1993, he was widely respected as a manager and had a studious approach to the game. Regardless of that, he had his share of run ins with Dale Scott.

Cito approached the mound during a mound visit, waited for Umpire Scott to approach and starts talking about pitches and the strike zone. Once again, Scott gave his standard reply for this situation, "Cito, we are not going to talk about that."

Gaston replied the same way that Sparky Anderson did in the above example, "The heck we aren't." He was then ejected from the game.

The one thing different about this ejection was that after he was ejected, Gaston said, "I'm sick and tired of this." He repeated the same thing emphatically to the umpire. Scott and Gaston had previous arguments and often were not on the same page, according to Scott. Gaston then aggressively said, "Meet me outside after the game and we will settle this once and for all." Gaston was insinuating a personal, physical confrontation. Scott, being the firm arbitrator that he was, told Cito that Dr Bobby Brown, the president of the American League and chief disciplinarian of the league would be thrilled to hear his comment and threat to umpires, as Scott wrote up in his required report. Gaston threw back an expletive about Dr Brown at that point. Scott said that Dr Brown would also be thrilled with that reply that would go into the report.

Just as a side note here, according to the actual MLB Official Rule book, Baseball Rule 8.04 states:

a.   The umpire shall report to the League President within twelve hours after the end of a game all violations of rules and other incidents worthy of comment, including the disqualification of any trainer, manager, coach or player, and the reasons, therefore.

b.   When any trainer, manager, coach, or player is disqualified for a flagrant offense such as the use of obscene or indecent language, or an assault upon an umpire, trainer, manager, coach or player, the umpire shall forward full particulars to the League President within four hours after the end of the game.

Umpire situations are a few more instances of communication in *Baseball Confidential*. We as fans would have liked to have heard these exchanges in real time. We can now bring those to light.

Scott had a way of defusing or at least handling different types of umpire/player/manager situations. One time, he had a situation where the catcher called time. The catcher joined the manager for the standard mound visit. The opposing team had runners on base and the next batter at the ready, next up. The batter, coyly, asked Umpire Scott, "What does this new pitcher usually throw?" Scott's reply was he usually throws doubles and triples. That surprised the batter as he said he would take a triple. This endeared the umpire to the player, put a little humor in a tense situation and probably defused in advance any potential conflict.

Managers manage umpires as part of their management game. Lastly, Scott had a situation where a manager signaled for a pitching change (after his mound visit). When that happens, the umpire usually retreats to his position to get ready for the next at bat. As the manager reported the lineup change to Umpire Scott, he said, "Dale, just so you know, this incoming pitcher throws a lot of strikes. Seriously, at his last bullpen session, he didn't throw one ball."

All Scott would say back is, "I guess we will find out."

It turns out that this was a common approach with managers as it happened more than once with Scott. Umpires and the ensuing interaction and communication are just part of the game. That's Baseball!

Position Players

Bret Boone – Position Player Awareness

We've already said that it's not only catchers, coaches, and managers that make mound visits.

Infielders make mound visits. Infielder mound visits are less these days, because of new mound visit rules and the limitations per team, associated with them. Before those rules and limitations were in place, infielders made way more mound visits, with and without the catcher, manager or pitching coach.

There are situations where there is great benefit for infielders to join the mound visit. It could, as you will read, be a situation where there is an obvious bunting situation to move a runner or even score a run, the infielders then, along with the pitcher and catcher have to coordinate a defensive strategy. You will hear of the infield bringing in the corners and the catcher signaling where he would throw when fielding a bunt.

Some of this is a bit different in today's times with the limitation on the number of mound visits a team can make during a game; however, they still happen with other position players. Typically, it is a leadership initiative that a position player takes on that pushes him to make a mound visit.

Bret Boone was one that initiated mound visits from his position as a second baseman. Bret Boone was one of those team leaders in his time. Bret Boone had a good sense of baseball awareness. This applied to his performance but because of his experience, he could use it to teach younger players.

Bret Boone is the grandson of Major League Baseball infielder Ray Boone, the son of catching great Bob Boone and the first third-generation big league player in the Major Leagues. As it stands now, the Boones are one of four families to have three generations of major league players. Bret Boone is a three-time All-Star, four-time Gold Glove winner, and two-time Silver Slugger Award winner. He is the brother of Aaron Boone, manager of the New York Yankees. Given all of that, his baseball perspective and perspective on player communication is invaluable.

Before the days of mound visit limitations, it was not uncommon for infielders to join in or even initiate mound visits. Often, they would discuss defensive shifts and strategies, base coverage and more, related to infield play.

Bret relayed much about his mound visit approach to *Baseball Confidential* and situations that he was involved in.

At first, Bret said unless he didn't need to be part of a mound visit, he wasn't there however, and he admittedly said he was pretty much present in most mound visits, whether initiated by him or not. As an experienced infielder, he could tell when a catcher was making a mound visit to calm a pitcher down, give him a break or a breather, he would let the two players have that meeting for themselves. That being said, Bret did say that he initiated mound visits to give pitchers a break. Most of his mound visits amounted to less important discussion, certainly less strategic and more relaxing for the pitcher. He might even tell a joke or something to break the monotony or pressures in a pitchers mind.

There are mound visits; however, those are way more strategic and attuned to the moment of the game. He would, many times, be there to review situations like what runners are on base, especially, a second base runner, right at Bret's position.

Bret talked about sometimes having a pitcher on the mound that didn't like to initiate a pickoff move at second base. Some pitchers just don't like to throw to second base. He mentioned that sometimes the opposite happens. Some pitchers are overzealous about throwing to second for a pickoff. As a second basemen, through position player, pitcher, and catcher communication, the second baseman can put of a pickoff sign. The second baseman has to be part of that arrangement as he will be fielding the throw from the pitcher. When he puts on the pickoff sign, his goal is not necessarily to pick the runner off. Once in a while, a tag might get a runner out. That's almost luck in the second baseman's mind especially given the fact that their purpose is to keep a runner closer to second base. He really wants to prevent that runner stealing third base or thinking he can steal. Keeping him close to second prevents the runner from getting another step or two toward third in case of a base hit. That step or two could be the difference between, as Bret describes it, a bang-bang out play at home plate or a bang-bang safe play. That's the whole reason for the attempted pick off. He wants to send a message to the runner that they, as the defenders, are aware of him. It's that simple.

Now back to that pitcher that doesn't like to throw to second for an attempted pick off. This could be another scenario that initiates a mound visit. If there is a runner on second and one of those pitchers is on the mound, that leaves the defender in a pickle. In that case, Bret would go to the mound and say, "Listen, we have something to do here. I know you don't like to pick, and we are not going to pick him off, but I don't like the lead he is getting, and we cannot allow him to steal third in this situation. What are we going to do to combat that?" Maybe the pitchers and Bret suggest a step off before the pitch, or successive step offs or a fake pickoff attempt. The goal is to disrupt the runner's rhythm at second base.

Bret talked about one player that sticks in his mind, Chone Figgins. Figgins was a former third baseman and outfielder playing for the Los Angeles Angels of Anaheim, Seattle Mariners, and Los Angeles Dodgers. Figgins was a utility player, playing all the non-pitcher, non-catcher positions. He was also very fast. Bret said Figgins used to drive him crazy when on base. He was one of those players that just had a knack of stealing third base. Usually, there was nothing Bret could do to hold him on or distract/disrupt him. Unless the pitcher cooperated with the situation, Figgins was destined to steal third base. He had to give a slide step, a fake or as Bret says, 'a look.' Those situations happen and it takes, sometimes another mound visit to plot the approach.

Most of the time, besides holding a runner on second, Bret goes into his pitcher to suggest, "How we doing? You alright? I'm just buying some time here for you. Let's settle down and get this guy." Sometimes, as Bret says, he will talk about something stupid. Maybe they will talk about somebody in the stands or something that happened in the stands, something funny or even make fun of the pitcher, anything to get his mind off of a tenuous, pressure packed situation. With Bret's experience, he knew of something that would make the pitcher laugh. He just wanted to break up the monotony and seriousness of the situation. Bret might even be told to shut up in that situation, but his goal is accomplished because the pitcher then would have his mind off the seriousness. That worked more times than not.

Here is another unique situation to the second base position and the related strategic input. There were times when Bret, as the second baseman, had an inkling that a runner on second base was picking the pitching signs and relaying them to the batter. Bret would visit the pitcher and say, on this mound visit, I'm not sure, but I think he is picking up on your signs. Let's mix them up and see how the hitter responds. They may mix up the signs and go completely backward. If the hitter is expecting a breaking ball and is thrown a fast ball and takes a swing, there is a good indicator at that point that signs are being stolen by that runner on second. The second baseman then has a problem with the runner on second. Any knowledge, competitive or otherwise, is an advantage.

Usually, when there is a congregation on the mound by all infielders, catcher, pitcher, and coach, it is a big situation, a strategic situation along with the pitcher struggling. The coach/manager talks about what everyone is thinking and sets the defensive strategy and/or offering a scouting report on the upcoming hitter.

Bret and fellow shortstop, Hall of Famer, Barry Larkin were the baseball equivalent of two peas in a pod. Both players, with their level of experience in the game and playing together had the freedom to decide what they wanted to do to cover certain situations. Manager at the time, Davey Johnson would often look at the two of them and ask them what they wanted to do. Their replies were usually that they wanted to focus on turning double plays. If it was a runner on first and third, with one out and the game was on the line, the two of them would be playing at double play depth and took their chances at turning a big double play. Their decision usually was not to bring the infield in and shorten it to attack a single runner. Bret's typical response to his manager was that they were turning the double play. Anything hit his way, he would turn it and his teammate felt the same. There were times that if a fast-running hitter was at the plate and runners were on, that unless they got the absolute perfect routing double play ball, they were not going to turn the double play and couldn't risk going down one run, all because they thought they could be double play turning superheroes. Players have to be smart in these situations. Bret says you have to put the ego away and be realistic. The focus always is winning the game. His obligation is to his team with a focus on winning, at all costs. Nothing else, including egos, matters.

This is contrasted with situations where it is the ninth inning, a cold night, and the field is playing slow. Their goal then is to cut the runner off at the plate, so that will be discussed many times on the mound. The benefit is that all hear it and are on the same page.

Sometimes and today, most times, managers visit the mound to pull a pitcher. Sometimes, they don't. Some managers will admit after the game that they might have been in the middle of that decision. They visit the mound to check on their pitcher, give him a look, up and down, assess his body language or look for a telling gesture. Then they make their decision to leave them in or not. Living together as a team with all players for 162 games a year, players and especially the manager learns how to ready his players. Managers can tell when the pitcher has had enough.

Most pitchers will not want to give up the game or ask to be taken out. They will tell the manager they have the situation in hand. Bret did mention, those are egos talking. That's the way ballplayers are wired. They all want to compete. Sometimes, a manager would ask Bret what he thought about a pitcher. Bret would say he's done or he's good let him stay in. He was careful though not to humiliate a pitcher in front of his manager, but he did have to be honest. He did not want to affect the livelihood of another player. It's eventually the manager's decision. Input is nice but only one person is responsible for the decision.

After all this, Bret still says mound visits don't really involve big things. They do talk about where they are having dinner after a game or make fun of something down the right field line (fan or player) or something humorous. He classified these as 50% of the mound visits.

Defensive strategies, mound visit conversations, strategies on hitting against certain pitchers are what players thrive on. Bret did. He said those are all the cool parts of baseball, the game inside the game. Those are the things past players, like him, miss. They don't miss chasing sliders off the plate or facing a pitching powerhouse trio like Maddux, Smoltz, and Glavine. They do miss the mound visits and the humor. They miss the intricacies of the game, figuring out a problem then having a strategy.

Other Position Players Making Mound Visits

The interest of most fans is related to what conversations are like when a catcher, coach or manager visits the pitcher's mound in the middle of a game. *Baseball Confidential* is looking at that in depth, behind the scenes, to satisfy the curiosity of many fans.

A lot of the in-depth uncovering of mound visits has been related to catcher conversation with pitchers or coaches and managers conversing with a pitcher, usually in a struggling situation.

It's not only catchers, coaches, and managers that make mound visits. Other position players either initiate those conversations or join in with catchers and coaches. That is a bit different in today's times with the limitation on the number of mound visits a team can make during a game; however, they still happen with other position players.

Roughned Odor was a second baseman for the New York Yankees. He loved making mound visits. Usually, second basemen aren't the most logical choice player to participate in mound conversation, but Odor would beg to differ. Sure, infielders join in on mound conversations, especially when discussing defensive strategies or during a pitching change. Odor includes those as well as just about all other mound visits while he is on the field.

Roughned is Venezuelan by descent and speaks good English. His visit sometimes could be acting as an interpreter depending on the pitcher. He will, though, visit the mound even when there are no language barriers and no translation needed. Today, many teams have a language translator that now is allowed on mound visits. Sometimes, Odor initiates the mound visits but again, today's rules have changed to limit mound visits, so players have to be more strategic about their mound visits. You can bet, though, that when the catcher initiates a visit, Odor will join in.

He hasn't said it formally, but Odor wanted to show leadership qualities. Mound visits show support as well as keeping him in the loop of game and batter strategies. Infielders are many times part of strategies. Defensive ploys are discussed in anticipation of upcoming batters or in reflection of scouting reports.

Jazz Chisolm, Jr has said that Derek Jeter advised him to join in as many mound visits as possible if not all of them. You can bet Jeter was part of most mound visits.

Probably in most cases, Odor wanted to either be part of the strategy (defensive) or at least know about it. Bunt plays, shifts, base coverage, and more often discussed during a mound visit. Infielders, like Odor need to be on the same page.

Lastly, anyone with a devout interest in baseball wants to know what is being said between players, with coaches and managers and other players. It's a natural fan curiosity. Odor had that same curiosity as a player at times, so he joined in at the mound.

Mound Visit Strategy and Communication

Mound Visit Strategy – Communication and More

In *Baseball Confidential,* there is a lot of talk about mound visit conversation: understanding strategy, psychology, motivation, communication and more. The one thing, though, that any pitcher will say is that they would prefer not getting a mound visit during a game. Susan Slusser of the *San Francisco Chronicle* has shared with me that Sonny Gray, now with the Minnesota Twins described it as, "The best-case scenario, you don't get a mound visit. That means you haven't had a long inning, you're not in trouble. The best games involve *no* mound visits."

But given the state of the game and the fact that mound visits are still a part of the game, are strategic and have a place, we will dig into more of that private conversation that we as fans are always wanting to hear more of. We do wish that players, coaches, and managers wore microphones, so we could hear firsthand those conversations. That's not realistic, so we will rely on these interviews and reports of what actually goes on. Slusser of the *San Francisco*

Chronicle has a great term for these visits. She terms them as an under-the-radar but fascinating aspect of baseball: the mound visit.

She actually has called mound visits an art, usually when an opponent is threatening. Stories about those visits and that art show up often; some good, some not so good.

Mound visits can be psychological in nature. I prefer to use the classification as strategic as much as psychological. When to go to the mound, why go to the mound, what information or direction can be shared and what suggestions are offered relating to pitching adjustments. Sometimes, the strategy is to slow the pace of the game, give the pitcher a breather, and interrupt the momentum of an opponent or even stalling to allow a bull pen pitcher time to warm up.

A lot of conversation in baseball, before, during, and after a game depends on many different strategies, scenarios, planning and actual plays during the game. Much of it really boils down to three things: one is the pitcher, one is the catcher and the other, is strategies and tactics.

Scott Emerson, Oakland A's pitching coach at the time offered his thoughts on the thinking behind a mound visit: 'This guy is all over the place, and I've got to make a trip because he's not throwing strikes.' Emerson is quick to point out. "But the worst thing to do is to go out there and say, 'Just throw a fastball down the middle and let them hit it.' That usually ends up being a mistake.

Emerson learned from that early mistake. He was coaching a former Oakland A's minor league pitcher and offered that very advice. Before his return to the dugout after the mound visit, the opposing batter had hit a home run. Emerson admitted to himself that he would not do that again. The pitcher followed directions, literally, threw it right where the coach had told him to throw it and you see what happened. He admits it was a mound visit learning experience.

The right communication is key. Clarification is desired but not at the expense of confusion. That happens. Catchers, coaches, pitchers, and managers all have to be on the same page.

Current San Diego Padres manager, Bob Melvin recalled a time when he was catching pitcher Mark Grant with the San Francisco Giants. Roger Craig was the manager. Craig, in his day, played for 12 seasons (1955-1966) followed by a successful post-playing career as a pitching coach and manager.

Melvin as the catcher got the signal from manager Roger Craig for a pitchout. The Giants were playing the Phillies. The count on the batter at the time of the pitchout was three balls and two strikes with a runner at third.

Melvin tells it so well. "I looked over at Roger, sat there for a moment, looked over again," Melvin said. Melvin states that his manager was fuming. Sometimes, that what managers do.

Melvin continues as he was confused, "I went to the mound, and said, 'Hey, Mud, correct me if I'm wrong, but isn't a 3-2 pitchout a walk'?" The manager made the pitchout call because he anticipated a Phillies batter attempting a squeeze bunt. Any question of his strategy made him more furious.

Melvin's mound visit broke the pace and rhythm of the game so much that Craig took the pitchout signal off. He was still irate. Pitcher Mark Grant wound up walking the batter anyway. That mound visit was full of confusion. Too bad the result wasn't any better. At least the run never scored.

Sonny Gray, referred to earlier is quick to point out that "Most of the time when they come out, you're not doing well, so you're not in a good mood." That's where psychology of a mound visit enters the picture.

Slusser reports on a conversation with Chris Smith, former Oakland A's pitcher and currently, a pitching coach in the Oakland Athletics organization. In learning of his mound visits, it's a little less stringent and sometimes humorous. His fellow catcher teammate Bruce Maxwell said, "He's about the goofiest guy I've ever caught. He'll go, 'Yeah, they're hitting me hard, aren't they? Hey, let's not do that again.' He has a comeback for everything. It's awesome."

We have heard it in abundance, but Smith agrees with us when he says that's the standard line most pitching coaches or managers say is, "I'm just giving you a breather."

Chris Smith's reply in those instances is usually something like, "You know what, I don't need a breather – I need Billy Wagner's fastball or Trevor Hoffman's changeup right now."

Smith also tells about the coach/manager making and mound visit and stating as a matter of fact, "Hey, what's going on out here?"

Smith's reply was classic, "Well, I'm obviously in some trouble. You're out here for a reason. You're not checking to see where I'm going to dinner." Sometimes, that initial question from the coach or even a catcher is, "Hey, what do you want to do here?"

Smith has been known to say, "I don't know! I want to be in the dugout! I don't want to be here. I want to go home! Bases loaded and no outs, you know?"

Humor defuses. Humor helps with a pace. Humor works sometimes.

Scott Emerson, the current Oakland A's pitching coach uses humor when appropriate. He tells the story that one time in the minor league, he made a mound visit. Ben Fritz, current bullpen coach for the San Diego Padres and pitcher at the time, saw Emerson approaching for his visit. The minute he crossed the foul line on his way to talk, Fritz yelled out, "I love you, Emo." Emerson will admit that Fritz's offering took the edge off of what was about to be communicated by Emerson. Emerson relented and said OK. "Let's go get 'em," turned around and retreated to the dugout. Humor worked.

Dusty Baker-Joe Ross – Clean Slate

In all of this mound visit conversation that we are peeking at behind the closed door, giving pitchers a breather or a break in the action is discussed. Joe Ross, pitcher for the Washington Nationals termed it best when he summarized what happened on one of his encounters on the mound with manager Dusty Baker. Joe clearly said that Dusty's move or lack of move provided confidence to Joe and more which is what led to his classification of getting a 'clean slate.'

The situation was that Joe Ross was pitching against the New York Mets. With no one out in the top of the third, while already getting beat 4-0, Ross had given up his fourth straight hit. Not the most ideal situation for a team that desperately needed a win at that point in the season. The Nationals were in the midst of a seven-game losing streak and their ace pitcher had just strained his back on the way to the DL list, thus the desperation to win one. With that desperation and the hit barrage by the opposing team, out of the dugout pops manager, Dusty Baker. Usually, at this point in the game, in similar situations, Dusty would have sent pitching coach Mike Maddux to the mound for the necessary conversation with the pitcher. Dusty decided that he wanted to make this visit. As it turns out, he had a motive. Call it ulterior or otherwise but Dusty had a purpose. To the casual fan, this looked like a ticket to the showers for Joe Ross. To further substantiate the hunch of replacement was the fact that Dusty almost never made a mound visit without replacing the pitcher. Everyone thought that his streak of replacement would continue here. Everyone also knew this was a game Dusty didn't want this game to get away to the point of no return to victory.

Dusty's normal course of action would be to extend his hand as a gesture to ask for and then take the ball. That's exactly his pattern and what he did for the first 75+ games of the season that year (2016).

Eddie Matz, senior writer for *ESPN* at time described it best.

Baker stood face to face with Ross, just like he did back in spring training after Ross' first bullpen session. At that time, Baker pulled the young pitcher to the side and gave him the tip of pulling the brim of his cap lower on his head to project a tougher, more rugged look to a batter. Thirty-three thousand fans were watching Baker intently to see what his move would be. Dusty didn't care about the fans when it came to managing for a win. He was on that mound to manage a situation and a pitcher.

Dusty, almost three times the age of his floundering pitcher stared intently into Ross' eyes. This stare, Dusty's mannerisms, his relationship with players allowed him to do what he did best. That was to 'connect' with his pitcher.

According to *ESPN* writer Matz, here is how the conversation went. Dusty said to pitcher Ross, "The ball is yours." You could almost see Ross do a big whew, of relief. He was all of a sudden more at ease. Dusty was letting his pitcher know that his evening wasn't over yet. Dusty went on and said, "Just attack the hitters." It almost didn't matter what was said since Ross already knew he was staying in the game and already motivated to do whatever Dusty told him to do. Dusty further encouraged by saying, "I got your back, but now it's time to go to work. They don't get any more after this." Dusty clearly chose a motivational approach vs. a replacement or even and adjustment approach.

Dusty's words were simple. His action was evident. The effectiveness was spot on.

The Mets, at that point, prompting Dusty's mound visit were on the verge of breaking open the game. Ross, hearing Dusty's words and connecting retired the next three batters ending the opposing threat. He then retired the next three batters after that in the next inning and lo and behold did it again in the following inning.

Joe Ross was eventually replaced after a six-inning stint. Baker attributed his pitcher's comeback performance as one that fired up the rest of the team. The Nationals went on to win the game 11-4. After Dusty's mound visit and motivational chat, Ross' performance was stellar. Joe Ross gave all the credit to Dusty. Whether Dusty deserved all the credit, he didn't care. All he wanted was a win.

Dusty Baker was able to get Joe Ross focused and helped turn the tide of the game toward a win. As was said earlier, Dusty's move or lack of move provided confidence to pitcher Joe. Joe Ross clearly performed, won and was proud to perform all after getting a 'clean slate,' from his manager. Just one more reason to like Dusty Baker.

Every Mound Visit Is Different – Sport's Most Visible Coaching Moment

Sometimes, mound visits happen late in the game during prime time for relievers but sometimes, mound visits come very early in the game. If that happens, things are usually in dire straits. That happened in a Thursday, May 2nd 2014 game where the San Diego Padres were playing the Cincinnati Reds at Great American Ball Park in Cincinnati. Pitcher, Tyson Ross was on the mound for the Padres.

Ross took his position on the mound, threw his compulsory warm up pitches and began his inning. Things did not start well. He walked the first two Cincinnati batters to the plate. His pitches were moving like they were in the bullpen and during warm-ups, but command of his pitches was absent. That is a death knell for a starting pitcher.

Opposing batters can just stand in the batter's box and watch; watch for pitches wild or in the dirt. Lo and behold, Ross walked the third batter up to load the bases. Up from the dugout comes Padres pitching coach, at the time, Darren Balsley to make that very early mound visit. Call it a trot, jog, or brisk walk across the infield. At any rate, pitching coach Balsley had to go rescue the situation.

Usually, these types of mound visits, especially this early and with a lack of command, are to calm a pitcher down, break up his rhythm (or lack of in this case) or to give him a reset. That was Balsey's mission. Ross admitted after that game according to Dennis Lin, writing for the *San Diego Tribune* then, that Balsey's visit, albeit early in the inning/game, "He calmed me down a little. He just told me to get back in the strike zone, just let the movement work."

The visit worked. Two pitches to the next batter resulted in a ground out. Ross eventually worked out of the inning, unscathed, all thanks to a timely, necessary baseball move – a mound visit. Lin called it an example of sport's most visible coaching moment. It truly was visible, and the coaching moment was timely and worked.

There is no handbook for mound visits. Some are simple, others are more complex. Some are breathers, others are very strategic and can include other infielders. Umpires like them brief but there is no set time limit or rule for how long a mound visit is. Coaches, catchers, and managers also prefer briefer visits. Conversation has to be direct, measured, and precise and many times, specific. All of this is different for every pitcher, every situation and every catcher, coach, and manager. Mound visits take an infinite number of forms.

Lin reported that Bud Black who was the Padres manager at that time, currently manager of the Colorado Rockies and a former pitching coach himself says, "Every mound visit is different than any one you've ever had."

In Lin's report, pitching coach, Balsey boiled down all of his mound visits into three distinct categories.

First, there is what Balsey refers to as the 'mechanical fix.' Many sources explain mechanics as a coordinated sequence of body movements and muscular forces that have an ultimate goal of high ball velocity and target accuracy. An effective pitching motion is dictated by an intricate relationship of increasing the speed of body segments speed starting from the ground up. Balsey estimates that a quarter of his mound visits have pitching mechanics as the primary subject of conversation. Also in this category, according to Balsey is the plan of attack for the next hitter at bat, a discussion of the game plan, probably talked about before the game. This is a chance for a refresher course on that plan.

Balsey's second category is the 'give the pitcher a break,' category. It doesn't matter at what point in the game this happens as it can come early as we learned or later in the game. Pitchers sometimes need their monotony broken up. Sometimes, they need to slow down and catch their breath. Sometimes, a mound visit can break the opposing team's momentum, some. There is nothing scientific about this category and the pitching coach knows how all pitchers react in all situations and is a good judge of when these should happen.

The third category, broken down by Balsey he calls an art within an art. It's common knowledge in pitching circles that no pitcher wants a mound visit, even for a breather. Many pitchers, however, will admit, usually later, that they appreciate the mental break. It's not mechanically related but psychological in nature. Pitchers have admitted that when things start to go awry, they rush, tend to go too fast, feeling like they want to end the bad situation as quickly as they can. Although a pitcher's mind is rushing a mile a minute, the solution is really they need to step back, reset, and assess things. That's all within Balsey's third category.

Mechanical adjustments are talked about but as many have said, coaching is best done between games not during a mound visit in the heat of the moment. Balsey talks of what he calls a gentle nudge vs. a cure-all approach. For example, "Remember this key, stay on top of the ball. One good pitch and you're out of the inning." This could be scripted as it is an often-used set of nudges.

Remember this, a mound visit is a coaching moment. There are plenty of instances where a manager or coach goes to the mound and rips his pitcher. That certainly, especially in today's times, is not very positive motivation leaving a pitcher's mindset at risk. Robbie Erlin, one of Balsey's pitchers stated, "He keeps your mind on the positive and what you are going to do, not what has happened." Nothing that has happened can be changed. Things only go forward. Balsey knows this and so do his pitchers, on the receiving end of his coaching.

In an early start in the 2014 season, pitcher Robbie Erlin had, what could be deemed, a rough outing. Balsey, his pitching coach, after Erlin allowed eight runs and a boat load of hits had a mound visit (he did end up pitching just over five innings). Balsey told his young pitcher, "Look, the ball is still coming out good. Just do whatever it takes and save the bullpen a little bit. Just trust your stuff." This is a mound visit with a strategic slant by Balsey, thinking of keeping his bullpen as fresh as possible. This mound visit also did wonders for Erlin's confidence, which is a huge coaching component, especially since it helped Erlin get through a couple more innings.

Lin reports that Balsey is a master of mound visits. He doesn't make a mound visit just for the sake of visiting the pitcher's mound. He purposefully leaves some pitchers alone. He knows that some of his veteran pitchers don't want him out there. His veteran pitchers know the job at hand is to focus. They know what to do on the next pitch, pitch by pitch. Veteran pitchers, when not performing, know why they are not performing and tend to make their own necessary adjustments.

In contrast for the younger guys who speed deliveries and pitches while losing focus need a different approach. As it's been said before, just a mention of slowing things down is all it takes. Balsey calls this a twenty-second timeout.

Bud Black, mentioned earlier, likes to combine a strategic visit to talk about how to approach a certain hitter at-bat with a conversation for all infielders who join in about a particular defense or alignment to employ.

Even though this belongs in the humor section, it truly is an example of every mound visit being different so we will touch on it here. Bob Scanlan, field reporter for the San Diego Padres and former pitcher who pitched mostly for the Chicago Cubs, Milwaukee Brewers, and four other teams. He recalled for reporter Dennis Lin, a game early in his career, where he was pitching in the ninth inning. This was only Scanlan's second year in the major league. He got the first two batters out in that inning, no problem. Then, whoops, he gave up two back-to-back hits. You know what that means. Out to the mound, trots pitching coach, Billy Connors. Scanlan was ready to have a clinic on pitching mechanics and delivery. The visit wasn't exactly like that. Connors told his pitcher to flat out get the final out. He told his pitcher he was hungry, wanted the game to end with that final out so that he could get to the post-game meal of lasagna waiting in the clubhouse. Scanlan threw his next pitch for a ground out, ending the game. Scanlan went on to say and still probably will say it today, "Anytime I get nervous, I just think about lasagna." You can thank pitching coach Billy Connors for that!

David Aardsma – Middle Inning Focus and Recalibration

Baseball players have lots of stories. They go through many experiences from college to the minor leagues and then the big show. A lot of stories would be expected with these varied paths. What I have found is that pitchers seem to have a lot more instances worth talking about. Some of the stories are serious, some are funny, and many are eventful and memorable. That was certainly the case in talking to former MLB pitcher, David Aardsma.

David Aardsma last pitched in the major leagues in 2015 with Atlanta. His best years were with the Seattle Mariners, where he performed mostly as a closer saving 69 games from 2009-2010. Saves were nice but most of the time, he filled the role of middle inning reliever in his seven club, nine-year, MLB history.

Aardsma, who is now the Toronto Blue Jays player development coordinator, is a former first-round MLB draft pick, led the Rice Owls to a College World Series championship in 2003, and took over first place in the all-time major league alphabetical listing, bumping the infamous Hank Aaron. You can bet a player with this track record will have stories.

In talking with David about mound visits with pitchers, he discusses much of what every other pitcher talks about, but he does offer a few twists. Realizing that there are many reasons for mound visits, he still says they can be peculiar. Aside from the peculiarities he said, ninety percent of the time the same things are talked about with every pitcher on every mound visit. Pitchers can repeat these messages and conversations in their sleep, they hear it so much: "You have good stuff, just throw strikes."

"It's time to get strike one."

"This batter is prone to pulling the ball to left field, all the time."

"Watch the runner on second base." Other situations are discussed but at the end of all this, David will say mound visits are usually made to give the pitcher a break and a breather.

David offered one of the better quotes related to this when he said, "Pitching is about slowing down and hitting is about speeding up." As pitchers (and batters) remember this, they will pace themselves accordingly. If they don't, they have to be reminded to slow down or speed up. For pitchers, this usually results in a mound visit.

David was reluctant to name names for his stories but finally did. Aardsma played his college ball for Rice University. He played for legendary coach, Wayne Graham. After 26 full seasons at the helm of the Rice baseball program, and 37 seasons as a collegiate head coach, Graham is known as one of the top baseball coaches in the country, having built a solid baseball program at Rice.

Graham did play in the major leagues before that for Gene Mauch's Philadelphia Phillies and for legendary Hall of Famer Casey Stengel and the New York Mets.

Aardsma was on the mound, in one of his college games. He was struggling a bit. He normally pitched well and was, at this point of his college career setting up to be in the top ten of the MLB draft. In fact, this was the year Rice won the national championship. Aardsma talked about a two-week stretch of games where the team did not play at a championship level. He said those two weeks were bad and he was one of the guilty ones contributing to that demise. He was on the mound and not pitching well. In this game, he was about to give up the chance for victory. Manager Graham calls time and walks out to the mound. He was furious. That seems to be characteristic of a lot of managers when a pitcher is underperforming. That was the case here. He told Aardsma point blank, "If I could shoot you in the head and kill you it would make me feel really good, but I can't do that because it's illegal." Graham turned around and walked back to the dugout, saying no more. Imagine a young kid, hearing that kind of message from someone they looked up to. Graham was extremely frustrated. He knew he couldn't say that message to anyone but Aardsma, so he did. That was harsh, but Aardsma pitched out of the inning and Rice won that game. Graham's mission of motivation, regardless of style, was accomplished.

Another instance with manager Wayne Graham came again during a time where Aardsma was again struggling on the mound. He admits to the struggling at that point but was at a point in his career that he was, 'starting to figure it out.'

Graham walked to the mound and told Aardsma, "You've got nothing and I'm going to take you out. Look down at the bullpen. Relief pitcher, Wayne Townsend is ready and warmed up (Townsend saw the mound visit and when Aardsma turned to the bullpen to see what Wayne Graham was referring to, Townsend waved to him)."

Graham went on and asked Aardsma, "Why shouldn't I bring him in?" Aardsma had the perfect reply now that it can be talked about. He told Graham that he had a changeup pitch ready and with the hitter coming up he could get him out with that pitch. Graham told Aardsma that he would give him one more pitch and then he would bring in reliever Townsend.

Here's where full disclosure comes in. Aardsma and the catcher looked at each other after Graham left the mound and the catcher said, "You haven't thrown a changeup all year." Aardsma knew that but that was his reply to his irate manager at that point in time. Aardsma proceeded to throw the best changeup pitch that he had ever thrown, and the batter fouled it off. Here's where the story gets even better. Wayne Graham started out of the dugout on his way to the mound just like he promised after that one pitch. The relief pitcher Townsend was running in from the bullpen to the mound. Before Graham crossed the foul line into the field of play, the umpire stopped him and told him not to go to the pitcher's mound. He could not have two visits in one at-bat, by rule. Graham yelled to Aardsma that this for sure was the last batter he would face and then Aardsma would be replaced.

Aardsma stayed in the game and threw another changeup. He struck the batter out and they were out of the inning. Aardsma was so fired up, very emotional, almost in an over-the-top manner and went into the dugout, very boastful and pointed (pointing is never suggested) and told his manager, "I got this."

Aardsma's pitching coach grabbed him, pushed him up against the wall and said, "You never talk to our coach like that." The message was sent and Aardsma calmed down outwardly, even though inside, he was still emotional and elated.

After the game, word was sent to Aardsma that manager Graham wanted to talk to him in his office. The immediate thought that went through Aardsma's head, at that time, was this was his final game ever. That's the message he was expecting from his manager. Fortunately, for David Aardsma, that wasn't the case. Manager Graham said to him, "I love what you did. I love that you yelled. I wanted that emotion out of you and I finally got it, don't ever do it again. Do it privately. Don't do it in front of the rest of team."

That was an even greater message sent to Aardsma that stuck with him the rest of his career. That coach wanted Aardsma to be a bulldog and that was his way of coaching him to that point.

Understanding mound visits and the communication that goes on during those has revealed many instances, some serious, some belligerent, and some very funny. This next incident is in that last category.

David Aardsma was pitching for the Seattle Mariners at the time. His pitching coach was Rick Adair, and his manager was Don Wakamatsu. Wakamatsu is a former catcher, coach, manager, and scout and liked to be in charge. Aardsma had a good relationship with the bullpen coach, John Wetteland, in addition to the other coaches mentioned. Aardsma called it a perfect storm set up to have a great pitching year and experience. He was in a game in a season where he was having a good year. In the game he was struggling a bit. He described it as kind of struggling and kind of not. He could be out of an inning with one swing and miss or a pop out of any kind, but he was beating himself. He had two on base and one out. Pitching coach Adair, made a mound visit. It was a one-run game. He was used to being visited in these situations. Adair approached Aardsma on the mound and all he said was, "Nod."

Aardsma, following his coach's directions, nodded. Adair said that was perfect. He said do that again, right now. Aardsma nodded. Adair then admitted that his manager, Wakamatsu wanted Adair to make the mound visit to offer words of wisdom. Adair didn't think he needed to but had to follow his manager's direction. He repeated again and asked Aardsma to nod one more time. He said, "You're killing it. Perfect!" He then started talking about observations of people in the stand, usually the good-looking girls, nothing baseball related. He finished by saying, "Go get 'em."

Aardsma knew that it was mostly about getting his mind off whatever he was doing that wasn't up to par. That mound visit took his mind off the pressure of the game and maybe baseball, in general. That was the purpose. Aardsma explains it as a recalibration. A coach can't visit and say, 'recalibrate.' No pitcher would be able to recalibrate with that instruction. Recalibration comes when taking their mind off the situation in total. Aardsma even said one coach told him to look at the flagpole. That's a total distraction and served its purpose.

There were a lot of commonalities with these stories that other pitchers have offered. It further emphasizes that it's a people game. It's a mental game and there are ways to make that better during games for pitchers. David Aardsma is that case in point.

Mound Visit Situations

Skip Schumaker – A Typical Mound Visit

Skip Schumaker shared, via USA Baseball, the various benefits of the pitching coach making a visit to the pitcher's mound during a game. USA Baseball (usabdevelops.com) is the national governing body for organized baseball in the United States and is a member of the United States Olympic Committee. Schumaker is a two-time World Series Champion, and the current new manager of the Miami Marlins. In addition to his two World Series titles, Schumaker was a member of the USA Baseball 2006 Olympic Qualifying team that won a gold medal in Cuba.

Schumaker talked of a situation in a game. The game was in the fourth inning, runners were on second and third bases. Schumaker is giving the manager's perspective here. He mentioned that in a situation like this, he likes the pitching coach to make a mound visit and talk to the pitcher, calm him down a little bit and letting the infielders know exactly what the coach wants them to do; maybe he wants to corner position players (first base and third base) up and the middle of the infield (second baseman and Shortstop) back. He describes this as the set up to play for just one run at most with the corners checking the runners and throwing out what becomes available and not giving up an easy run. Schumaker repeats that he never likes giving up the easy run especially early in the game where the lead is 3-0 and still a lot of game left.

Schumaker prefers the corner position players playing up in this situation and having the infield back forcing the hitter to try and manipulate the barrel of the bat in such a way to try to hit the ball up the middle. You have to avert the risk in case a batter hits one off of the end of the bat, squirting down first or third base. In this case, teams don't want to just give up an easy run.

In a situation like this, he repeatedly likes the corners back. That's the instruction and information he is hoping that his pitching coach shares during his mound visit. Of probably more importance as Schumaker describes, he is just trying to calm the pitcher down, knowing the situation, and trying to get outs with the lead. He wants his pitcher throwing strikes and be in a good spot. Aside from all of that there may be competitive scouting information on the upcoming hitter that can be discussed.

This is a quick description of a Schumaker coached mound visit but one that is very typical.

Mike Matheny – Mound Visits to Wainwright

No mound visit story telling would be complete unless there wasn't a mention of star pitchers. In this case, we are talking about Adam Wainwright of the St Louis Cardinals.

These aren't blockbuster revelations, but they do give a bit of a flavor of what goes on between catcher and manager. The manager in this case is Mike Matheny.

Mike Matheny, former manager of the St Louis Cardinals and Kansas City Royals also spent 13 seasons as a catcher for four MLB teams. Matheny won four Rawlings Gold Glove Awards as a catcher. Matheny's teams won one National League pennant and three NL Central division titles. These credentials certainly put him into position to understand pitchers, catchers, interactions, mound visits, strategies and more related to our national pastime.

One pitcher predominant during Matheny's time as St Louis Cardinals manager was Adam Wainwright. Waino, as his teammates call him and longtime Cardinal teammate Yadier Molina are the most successful battery in Major League history, having the most wins and starts as a battery. Imagine the mound visit conversations between those two, let alone with manager, Matheny.

For now, I will stick to conversations and communication involving manager Matheny.

It was mid-May in the 2016 season. The Colorado Rockies had just begun a nine-game road trip with a three-game series against the St Louis Cardinals were visiting the Colorado Rockies. It wasn't a huge rivalry even though the Cardinals have had their share of problems when visiting the Rockies. Any opposing team is a rivalry at some point even if at game time.

Adam Wainwright was on the mound pitching for St Louis. As has been written many times, Wainwright was having a good game even after a shaky beginning.

Wainwright pitched into the seventh inning in what was determined later, to be his best start of the 2016 season. It was in that seventh inning that Wainwright was showing signs that it might be time to end his outing.

Mike Matheny made a mound visit. Yadier Molina joined in. Basically, Matheny wanted to review the scouting report on the on-deck batter. He stated that he wanted to make sure all involved were clear on the upcoming hitter. It also gave Matheny to take a good look at his pitcher. Matheny knew, as most managers know, that if he asked Wainwright how he was feeling, the odds of the reply being that he wasn't good were extremely low. Matheny was of the mindset to still give pitcher Wainwright a chance to keep on pitching. Matheny stated this was the first conversation of that type for a start like this in the season with Wainwright. Matheny admitted that Wainwright didn't like mound visits like that but sometimes, as Matheny points out, it's good to get a breath. We continually hear breathing exercises in many mound visit conversations. It basically boils down to taking a breath, making sure everyone is on the same page for the next batter, and the game plan and just make sure the pitcher is in a good spot. Wainwright was and finally came out of the inning after two outs. The Cardinals preserved their lead and won 2-0.

Adam Wainwright said, in that game, his curveball was the best it had been all season (even though the season was still young). That spelled bad news for Colorado Rockies hitters, and smooth sailing for Wainwright. The St Louis Cardinals' preeminent pitcher threw six-hit ball into the seventh inning. It was by far his strongest start after a rickety beginning. Matheny knew when to make the mound visit and what to say. Winning was the result.

Mound visits don't always need to be overly strategic or complicated. There was another game at Busch Stadium where Matheny visited pitcher Wainwright late in the game. He didn't need to say anything. As he reported, he merely went to say a few words, or 'a little pep talk,' as Wainwright described it. Matheny didn't make that visit to ask Adam Wainwright, already at a pitch count of over 115 pitches to convince him that he still felt in good enough shape to finish off the inning. Matheny had already determined that his pitcher would stay. The visit was merely for motivation. Matheny told Wainwright how much he believed in him in the situation they were in and he believed his pitcher would get out of the tight spot they were in. Matheny left his ace in for one more hitter.

That pep talk worked. Motivation was in play, even for a veteran, experienced pitcher like Wainwright. He proceeded to strike out opposing batter, Yoenis Cespedes with the tying runs on base to close the seventh inning. Wainwright responded with a big whoop as he went on to celebrate a victory. The Cardinals beat the Red Sox 5-2 in that game. A small pep-talk sure helped.

Andrew Knizner – Keeping Things Loose on The Mound

St Louis Cardinals catcher Andrew Knizner told Sam Masterson of *NewsRadio 1120 KMOX* that usually when he gets to the mound, he's just trying to have a relaxing conversation. Knizner went on to say that overall, he tries to really know his pitcher. That seems to be the common job description thread of all the catchers we talk to. He proudly states that he tries to know what pitchers like him to go out and talk to them for whatever reason and which ones don't. Some don't want that mound visit, no matter what is happening. He says that he tries to understand what pitchers that he works with want him to make a mound visit and get on them a little bit, to have a sterner conversation and what pitchers like for him to visit and stay on the loose side. He prefers the looser conversations, and will many times go to the mound and just ask casually, what the pitcher is having for dinner that night or what he has planned to the off day tomorrow or even plans for later that same day/night. He likes, as he says, to keep things loose on the mound.

Luis Castillo and Derek Johnson – Knowing the Pitcher

On an early season, late May night, the Cincinnati Reds visited the Boston Red Sox in the infamous Fenway Park. Visiting Fenway was not in favor of the Reds. Cincinnati had a 0-11 record interleague play against the Red Sox since 1975. I paid particular attention to this since I am a huge Cincinnati Reds fan.

Spoiler Alert:

The Reds made history on this night as Cincinnati emerged victorious. It was historical as it was the first time the Reds had beaten the Red Sox at Fenway in the regular season. The last time the Reds won a game at Fenway Park was Game Seven of the 1975 World Series. Many call that Series one of the best World Series of all time.

Drew Koch reporting and writing about the Cincinnati Reds as the site expert at *Blog Red Machine,* revealed game details that included a comical mound visit that pitcher, Luis Castillo received from Reds pitching Coach Derek Johnson that night.

It was the bottom of the sixth inning with the Reds nursing a one-run lead due most in part to a throwing error by Boston Red Sox third baseman Rafael Devers. Needless to say, tensions were high in the close game and probably, in the back of the mind of some Red's fans, players, and management, history was on the line.

To that point, Luis Castillo was pitching what baseballers commonly refer to 'a gem.' The sixth inning started and Castillo proceeded to walk batter Jackie Bradley Jr on four straight, out of the zone, pitches. That was a rare feat for Castillo. Lo and behold, the next pitch was up and in with Castillo walking the next batter on four straight pitches. That put the tying run in scoring position with no outs.

Usually in that situation, with the game on the line, and being late in the game, a mound visit would be prompted by the catcher or pitching coach. Manager David Bell only made mound visits when changing pitchers. Sure enough, out of the dugout came pitching Coach Derek Johnson, making his way to the mound. He was joined by catcher Tyler Stephenson.

As Johnson approached, Castillo put his glove up to his face much like many do to shield their lip movement in conversation. In this case, however, it looked like Castillo was hiding a grin that was almost an audible laugh. He knew his comfort level. He knew his limits. He knew that this mound visit was needed.

Here is a breakdown of that conversation:

Johnson: "Are you ok?"

Castillo: "Yes."

Johnson: "Are you sure? It looks like you can't see the plate."

Johnson followed that short exchange with a few more motivating comments and left the mound; both still smirkishly grinning. They both classified it as a comical moment.

Did that mound visit work? Was that break in the action what Castillo needed? The visit and ensuing conversation seemed to help Castillo get back on track. The next batter he faced, Rafael Devers, grounded into a double play. Castillo then struck out the next batter, JD Martinez ending Boston's threat in the bottom of the sixth inning.

The point to a comical mound visit is that Derek Johnson knew his pitcher and knew him well. Derek Johnson is well-regarded as one of the best pitching coaches in the game. Having the relationships that he has with the Reds pitching staff helps him guide his pitchers and keep them focused, especially in tight or tense situations. In this case, a bit of humor is all that was needed.

As mentioned, the Reds broke their winless streak at Fenway as Cincinnati emerged victorious. It was historical as it was the first time the Reds had beaten the Red Sox at Fenway in the regular season.

Pitchers – Staying in The Game

Baker/Greinke – Staying in the Game

When you think of a mound visit, you think of a conversation, usually a two-way conversation between catcher and pitcher, pitching coach and pitcher, or manager and pitcher. In more modern times, a trip by the manager to the mound is done with a decision already made. Their minds are already made up. The manager usually knows that he is pulling the pitcher, replacing him with a reliever and making a quick and efficient change. Many managers even signal to the bullpen before he reaches the mound for the change. Not a lot of discussion at that point.

There are times when a player is either very passionate, very confident or very wishful that he thinks he should stay in the game. Sometimes, this attitude translates into a hot-headed disagreement and protest to the manager's actions. Jason Turbow mentions in *The Baseball Codes* that in these cases, balls are flipped into the air rather than handed off to the manager, threats are leveled, and feelings get scuffed. Other times, the opposite happens, communication takes place (two-way) and decisions are made jointly about what to do with the pitching/pitcher.

Game Four of the American League Championship Series was played in 2020, between the Houston Astros and the Tampa Bay Rays. This was the second postseason meeting between the Rays and Astros, a rematch of the 2019 ALDS.

Dusty Baker, premier manager of the Houston Astros was in the spotlight in the sixth inning of Game Four. There was one out and two opposing runners on base. Coming up to the plate for the next at-bat was Randy Arozarena, one of the hottest hitters in baseball at the time. Zack Greinke was pitching for the Astros. His game was going well, as planned except earlier in the game, he gave up a two-run home run to the next up batter Arozarena.

Baker made his mound visit. He went with the purpose of having a conversation with Greinke and his catcher, Martin Madonado. Greinke was about to pitch what is known as the third time through the order, third time in the game that opposing batters would go against Greinke, getting more familiar with him. Baker was ready for a change in pitching and bring in his warmed-up bullpen pitcher, Ryan Pressly. Pressly was yearning for his first assignment in the championship Series. Bringing him seemed like the most logical baseball move.

Spoiler Alert: That's not what happened.

Baker defied logic. Baker left Greinke in to pitch. Baker changed his mind because of two-way communication on the mound. Baker was heard to say after the game, "I usually don't change my mind, but I hadn't had my mind really; really made up until I got out there and I saw the look in Zack's eyes, and Maldy was adamant about: 'He can get this guy.' I said, 'OK, you've got it then.' It was more old school, doing the right thing that I thought was right."

Baker watched Greinke strike out the feared batter. That was followed by a Tampa Bay infield single to load the basis. Grienke's confidence soared, and he struck out the next batter to end the inning and the Tampa Bay threat. Houston went on to win the game, 3-2, their first win of the series. In this case, confidence from the pitcher, confidence that the manager had in the pitcher, and the trust between catcher and pitcher were all in play.

Aaron Boone and Gerrit Cole – I Don't Want to Come Out

On a warm, mid-July day in July 2021, Gerrit Cole, pitching for the New York Yankees pitched a complete game shutout in a 1-0 win against the Houston Astros.

As in many Gerrit Cole highlighted outings, a top moment revolved around a mound visit. With the tying run on base in the ninth inning, Yankees manager, Aaron Boone called time out and strolled to the pitcher's mound to talk with Cole. Boone wanted to talk, not necessarily ready to make a pitching change.

Cole saw his manager approaching and became animated, agitated, and vocal. He was literally yelling among his gathered teammates. He did not want to come out of the game at that point. Boone left him and Cole struck out the power-hitter Yordan Alvarez of the Astros. Cole had 129 pitches at that point, the highest pitch count of his career. Boone had reported that he didn't go out to the mound with the intentions of replacing Cole (at that time). He wanted Cole to be the one to pitch to Alvarez.

Boone shared with Craig *Carton* and Evan *Roberts* on their afternoon *WFAN* radio talk show, "When I went out there, I was comfortable with one more hitter. I wasn't going to take him out. I was just going to check the temperature. But that was gonna Alvarez's last hitter. I just wanted to make sure he was still good and sound, and as you saw he was pretty animated and ready to get after it."

The report was, there were plenty of F bombs thrown around in that animated outburst.

Boone interpreted that display as a hungry attitude to encourage the whole team to 'get after it,' finish the game and go for the win. Boone called it controlled emotion. That's a backhanded compliment to Cole in that situation.

Another Aaron Boone mound visit surprised the feisty Cole. It was Game Three of the 2022 ALCS, the Yankees against the Houston Astros. Boone pulled Cole out of the game in the sixth inning of that game. The Yankees went on to lose 5-0 allowing the Astros to go up 3-0 in the best of seven Championship series. That meant one more victory for Houston and the League Championship was theirs.

Cole, having a very good season, including his playoff performance had seven strikeouts on that day. That wasn't a bad tally given the situation. Boone didn't even visit to talk and decide as he has been known to do. Cole was removed by rule because the visit was Boone's second of the inning. By rule, the pitcher is to be released upon the second mound visit in an inning.

"I feel like a pitcher myself; I'm probably mostly surprised," Cole told reporters. "I always want to keep going. I was not ready to come out but to my knowledge, the second trip is what it is."

Boone explained his decision while acknowledging that Cole pitched well. He just wanted another pitcher to face the Astros at that time. The team was behind in runs and he was managing as best he could to not let any more runs in. He truly thought the Trivi pitches could result in weak contact or a playable ground ball.

With the Yankees loss, with or without Cole, the Astros were in position for a series sweep. Fast forward, that's exactly what happened as the Astros went on their way to capture the MLB Commissioner's Trophy for their eventual MLB World Series Championship.

Edwin Jackson – Not Coming Out-On the Way to a No-Hitter

There are many instances where pitchers tell their managers they are not coming out of a game. Almost every pitcher will tell his manager that he is fine and can still pitch, in every game. Ninety-five percent of the time, the pitcher is removed as the manager knows it's his decision and most of the time, the decision is made before he reaches the mound. Managers have left pitchers in the game after such pleas and have succeeded and many have failed greatly.

One that was successful was Edwin Jackson's 149 pitch, eight-hit no-hitter that he pitched for the Arizona Diamondbacks against the Tampa Bay Rays in June of 2010.

Jackson labored his way to the second no-hitter in Diamondbacks history. The key word here is 'labored.' No one would have predicted what happened after watching his first three innings. Jackson threw 70 pitches in that stretch, a very high number by comparable standards. Tampa Bay was challenged bringing men across the plate and left many on base during those three innings. He then settled down and the no-hitter buzz started happening.

The pitch count of 149 is almost unheard of for today's games. With that many pitches, Jackson had to plead his case. The Diamondbacks manager at that time was AJ Hinch. Hinch obviously had to visit the mound during that many pitches to check on his pitcher.

Jackson was steadfast. He told Hinch on a late inning visit, "I'm not coming out until I give up a hit or home run. You want to skip my next start, that's fine. Give me an extra day off, that's fine."

Jackson pondered that if he came out of the game without giving up a hit, he would have had a lot of 'What if?' questions. "What if I would have stayed in?" Fortunately for him, he didn't have to get to that point.

The no-hitter would have never happened if Jackson didn't feel, wasn't convincing with his manager and his manager was not in a listening frame of mind. All of those happened positively for Jackson. Nine innings, 148 pitches and a no-hit win, truly any pitcher's dream.

Humor in the Game

Zack Grienke – Fantasy Football Mound Visit

Whenever writing about pitchers, you try to think of those that are good, those with great success and those that are memorable. Zack Grienke is one of those pitchers. He is a likely Hall of Fame pitcher and described, often, as one of baseball's great characters.

Joe Posnanski, author of *The Baseball 100* was talking about Zack Grienke pitching. He said, as he described his pitching, "This was how easy pitching was for him. He didn't think about it. He didn't really have to work at it. He just threw the ball and hitters couldn't hit it, and that was all he knew and all he needed to know." Others have accused him of, 'playing in his own world.'

Many of the Kansas City Royals were sharing Zack Grienke stories for The Athletic, upon his return to the team a second time. Cal Eldred pitching coach for the Kansas City Royals told about a time when Grienke waved him out of the dugout in the middle of a game:

Eldred: "The first time he waved me out (out of the dugout), I was like, 'This guy is waving me out to the mound'?"

JJ Picollo who was the general manager of the Royals, chimed in: Nobody really knew what to do.

Eldred talked about being waved out and upon reaching Greinke, Greinke told him, "I don't really need anything. I just need a break."

General Manager Picollo said that all of a sudden, the entire infield started laughing.

Whit Merrifield a Grienke teammate at this time concluded after this exchange, "He's just different."

Zack Grienke has had his share of games in the spotlight, both good times and not so good times. He has pitched in big games and been a star. He also has been a goat as in goat, not meaning greatest of all time. Behind the scenes and under the skin, Grienke was probably a lot calmer on the pitcher's mound was much more peaceful and tranquil than met the eye or that the general fan knew.

This is his story as he told *MLB Network Radio.*

A little background for this story. Zack Grienke was heavy into fantasy football. He is known as being the type of person that when he chooses to get involved with something, he goes all in. He had a reputation with teammates, and fantasy league opponents as being a wheeler dealer. He gained the nickname, Trader Zack. He was always reconstructing his roster, making trades, and implementing strategies. He really was enjoying being as much the general manager as much as football. Zack was known as a guy who would work the clubhouse and work the league, for his fantasy football endeavors.

First, it was at a game at Dodger Stadium. Grienke was warming up in the bullpen, about ready to start the game, right before heading to the pitcher's mound to throw the first pitch, still in the bullpen. A.J. Ellis was Grienke's warm-up catcher in the bullpen and would be catching him during the actual game. Ellis tells, in his report to *The Athletic* that all of a sudden, Grienke stops his warm-up pitches and starts walking toward me, as I was crouched in my catcher position. I pop up from behind the plate and meet him before he gets all the way there. He looks at me and says, "I've been thinking."

I immediately thought right then, *I wonder what this is about. It could be about anything.* Grienke proceeds to engage Ellis, "I've been thinking. You guys have this quarterback injury issue going on now. I've got a ton of quarterbacks on my roster, and I noticed you've got a bunch of wide receivers on yours. I think we match up really well, so I think you guys should make a trade. We'll talk about it a little bit later." Of course, this had nothing to do with the game that was about to start. Grienke was in fantasy football mode. Grienke, then did a complete about face and walked back to the bull pen pitcher's mound.

The game started. Grienke was pitching mostly well. At an unexpected moment, A.J. Ellis made a mound visit. There were runners on base and the situation was more tenuous than situations earlier in the game.

Instead of discussing the game, the situation or pitching/game strategy, Grienke took the mound visit opportunity to propose a trade between his fantasy football team and Ellis' team. Ellis certainly didn't expect that as he trotted out to the mound. Ellis thought he was visiting the mound to talk pitch strategy or to give Grienke a breather. Grienke offered his catcher a fantasy football trade in the middle of a game. That's not something any one thought would be part of Baseball Confidential mound visit conversations.

Joe Posnanski goes on to write about Grienke, who was a runner up to Posnanski's *Baseball 100* and states, *He's Zack. He's just different. As a pitcher, he has invented and reinvented himself – he has mixed in at least nine different pitches, including a couple that probably don't have names. One time, he was pitching in Wilmington, and he called the catcher to the mound and said, "I want to throw the cutter here."*

The catcher said, "Do you throw a cutter?"

And Grienke said, "No. But I can."

The conclusion of all those who play and know Zack know that he's just wired differently, and everybody likes that wiring.

Baseball Humor at All Levels

Not a lot of strategic or even pep talk related conversations come to light for public consumption. *Baseball Confidential* is attempting to do that here and now. There are narratives, galore, told by every player, many of them imaginative and humorous. That is the case for those interviewed for *Baseball Confidential*. There is no doubt that there are high stress situations in all of sports and in baseball. Humor many times is a much-needed antidote.

There is a lot of behind-the-scenes communication in the game of baseball. We are trying to bring much of that to light. This section is written here primarily to bring a smile to your face; to show more of the fun side of the game.

Baseball is not only referred to as the great American pastime, but it is a source of many stories, facts, and some great humor. Whether it's the middle of the baseball season, in the heat of the playoffs or the dead of the offseason, you can count on one constant to keep you fulfilled: baseball humor!

This section is a departure from the usual and deliberate and shifts to the more humorous parts of baseball. It is a short account of something less mundane, more interesting, and humorous related to the mound visits, coach/player communication and the like that have been discussed. Many of the players and managers interviewed had funny stories. Those are incorporated in their reviews within. This is a special section to carve out a few snippets that are nothing but humor.

Every sport has its share of funny moments, times, and stories. Those with baseball, as we have learned, come surface in so many different ways at different times.

Baseball is a Funny Game as said by baseball legend Joe Garagiola in his book of the same title. Call it humor, call it antics, and call it joking around. The bottom line is that everything funny, whether on purpose or not is an attempt to make merriment out of the amusing game of baseball.

It's apparent from all of the mound visit stories, coach pep talks and player communication that language, storytelling, and antics can elevate baseball above the visual game and make it much, much more of an experience that all fans seek.

Mention humor and mound visits and many baseball fans will recant the famous mound visit scene in the movie *Bull Durham*, a 1988 romantic comedy baseball film. In the scene, Kevin Costner playing catcher Crash Davis makes a mound visit to chat with pitcher Nuke LaLoosh that actor, Tim Robbins portrayed. Nuke admitted his nervousness because his dad is at the game focusing his eyes on every pitch. During the mound visit, all members of the infield join in to either listen in or offer their own two cents worth, some baseball related some not. Here is the summary of the mound visit by Crash Davis, played in the film by Kevin Costner, when the managers asked what was going on in all of the discussion:

"Well, Nuke's scared because his eyelids are jammed and his old man's here. We need a live roo—is it a live rooster? We need a live rooster to take the curse off Jose's glove. And nobody seems to know what to get Millie or Jimmy for their wedding present. Is that about right? … We're dealing with a lot of sh__." *—Crash Davis (Kevin Costner), summarizing a meeting at the mound in Bull Durham.* The pitching coach played along and suggested candlesticks as a nice gift (for Millie or Jimmy) and suggested to find out where they are registered and get a place setting or maybe some silverware. He concluded his mound visit by saying let's go, let's get two.

That's just the tip of the iceberg when it comes to mound visit humor. It happens in the major leagues, more in the minor leagues and a whole lot in little league.

Let me introduce a little league coach who uses humor in his coaching mission or at least in his mission to send messages to overzealous parents and coaches in the little league sport of baseball.

Scott Bergin is a baseball coach from Texas that is making a difference in his community. He pokes fun at the all-too serious nature of youth sports by creating pregame speeches and mound visit conversations, bordering on senseless parody, still in jest. Remember, there is humor in baseball.

Coach Scott has a mission to knock a few of those hyper-competitive coaches down a peg before their next game or next coaching session. His videos and interjection of humor has taken on a life of its own in his community and have popular place on the popular Internet video channel, *YouTube*. Just check out how many views they get. We will capture here some of the instances he portrays as we further look at humor in baseball.

Scott will reconcile the importance of winning or losing. As he told the *Washington Post* in a feature article about him, "I want my players to want to win and I'd be lying if I said I didn't care either. It's just finding that balance so that you can achieve all your goals at once. My goal is to get kids to think: 'I can't wait for the next season; I want to play more.' That's the point of youth sports, I think, to create a life-long passion for the game."

Scott goes on to justify his thinking by stating, "When you're coaching five-year-olds, the majority of them don't even know if they won or lost. Most leagues don't keep score, but ours did because the coaches and parents complained. So, really, at that point, who is the game for?"

In response to his frustrations of the game drifting away from its primary purpose and primary audience, Bergin began creating playful and humorous *YouTube* videos, in parody. His work became well known and talked about in Houston Little League communities. Although Scott insists, he was just trying to provide a humorous approach to the madness, he said it felt good to show other coaches what is they may look like as they lose sight of their purpose.

The best way to frame all this up is that Scott Bergin really works hard to create experiences to enjoy.

Scott reiterates one, final time: *"Ultimately, without a doubt, I want players to leave with a new-found passion. That sounds cliche, but it's not. I truly try to coach so that kids end the season not thinking about wins or losses, but saying: 'Wow, that was so much fun, I can't wait to do it again'."*

Let's look at some of Scott's humorous creations.

We will start with a pre-game pep talk. Remember, Scott does this to hopefully make others see that their thinking might represent the wrong purpose of little league baseball.

Ok, last game of the season, eyes on me. I want to make sure you guys remember what our goals are when we step on this field. Jackson with an X, what is one of our goals when we step on this field? To do your best. Not even close. Blayne what is one of our goals – to do our best and try to win. No, but I do like the second half of that. Did we learn anything this season? Our goals are to hit dingers, disgrace the pitchers family, make the other players cry and stomp their butts into the ground. Does everyone understand that? There are two types of people in this world. There are winners and there are losers. Just so we are clear, every time we step on this field, our goal is to be a winner. If your dad says it doesn't matter whether you win or lose, just as long as you have fun, then I hate to say then your dad is a loser. Let's get our hands in. That team is pretty good, but we are gooder. Hands in. gooder on 3. 1, 2, 3 Gooder!

These are short mound visit comments made by Coach Scott as he continues use sarcasm and humor to make his overall point (to parents and other coaches):

- "Did I seem wasted during tryouts? Because I can't figure out how you made it on this team."
- "Clearly practice doesn't seem to be working."
- "This is why everyone talks about as soon as you leave the dugout."
- "Did you take your Adderall this morning because you're acting kind of freaky out here'"
- "I knew you couldn't do it."
- "You don't suck. It's like you have bad luck every time you step on the field."
- "Dude you are destroying the backstop. The league is probably going to make us pay for a new one."
- "You do see the trend out here, right? Every time you are on the mound, we get murdered."
- "Martinez (coach stumbling, challenged with the Spanish language) *tu lansare welgis";* Player: "Coach I speak English."
- "If I end up in rehab this season, it's all your fault."
- "I heard you were the worst player on your last team as well."
- "Have you been tested for dyslexia?"

- "I'm sitting over there in the dugout holding my breath just trying to pass out."
- "Ok, hand me the ball and go to right field and don't ever come back."
- "Over 1.3 million little league players in the United States and I got stuck with you."
- "It's ok to suck once in a while but don't you think you are overdoing it?"
- "You do know that you're supposed to be throwing strikes out here, don't you?"
- "Look at it this way. You are not the worst little league pitcher on the planet you just better hope that the kid that is never quits. I take that back; you are the worse."

Pre-game speeches in baseball happen more at the college and Little League Levels. They do happen at the pro levels but generally less often. The following is the pre-game speech that most little coaches wish they could give, like Scott Bergin.

It's not clear if this speech had the same effect as Drew Brees' motivational pre-game pep talk for the LSU baseball team. Brees' impassioned speech was probably a primary motivator for LSU's leadoff hitter, centerfielder Dylan Crews, that day, to hit a 433-foot home run off the top of the stadium's scoreboard in the team's first at-bat of the day. Those are the kind of pep talks and results that all coaches dream of.

Here is Coach Scott Bergin's pre-game motivation:

Coach Scott: Ok, guys, EYES ON ME, AND I NEED SILENCE.

Don't move, don't blink, don't move a molecule.

I want to make sure you guys understand what our objective is when we take the field tonight.

Player Jack: To have fun and be a good sport.

Coach Scott: Holy mother of God on earth and in heaven, both at the same time, that is not even close. Our goals are not to be out here and have fun and be good sports and try and do our best and all that crap.

Our goals are to win. We are going to win at all costs.

Who are we playing tonight?

Team Response: THE HOOKS

Coach Scott: I'm pretty sure they can hide their own Easter eggs.

We are going to serve them up a plate of humiliation tonight.

We are going to get a big and early lead and we are not going to let up.

We are going to pummel them at all costs.

We are going to pummel, pummel, and pummel.

We are going to dominate and hammer them.

I want you to play dirty if you have to; just don't get caught.

Connor, you are on the hill tonight and I want you serving up nothing but gas; the powerful explosive gas that you get when you eat a whole bag of apricots by yourself.

That's the kind of gas we are throwing tonight.

I don't want to see any laziness out on the field tonight.

I promise you that if I look out and see one of you twerps taking a standing siesta, digging holes, I promise you, there will be an amber alert out for you before the end of the game.

Does everyone understand that?

We are going to turn out cleats sideways and download our cleats into the HOOKS fart chimneys today.

Does everyone understand; are we all on the same page?

We can steal their lunch money. Our objective is to steal their lunch money.

We are not losing.

Hop up.

We are the NUTS; we are Deez NUTS and we are dominating tonight Connor, Loud, NUTS on 3 Deez Nuts on 3, 1, 2, 3, Deez Nuts!

Side Note: No information is available on the outcome of the game.

Growing up in the 1960s, we would run and hunt for a flat field, throw down some makeshift bases (hub caps, shirts, pieces of wood) and create a field of play for our favorite game: baseball.

We didn't always have fancy uniforms. We didn't keep stats and there were no end-of-the-season awards. We were there to live our childhoods and just have fun. There were no uniforms. There were no records. There were no statistics. There were no trophies. We just had fun.

A lot has changed since our childhood days many years ago. Little league sports have developed and are now the central focus of many lives. One of the more controversial parts of that development to help with any controversy or fairness is the development of the participation trophy and now the two sides and debates of the pros and cons of the awards.

The debate ranges from whether a generation of younger Americans are spoiled, needed, and feel entitled.

Many of the older generations feel and believe today, that the younger generation is entitled and doesn't have the work ethic, creativity, discipline, accountability, or initiative they had. Others will add will, determination, grit, and hard work to this. This debated against those that believe that any recognition will help self-esteem.

Regardless of which side you are on, this portrayal by Coach Scott Bergin will offer the humor that exists in baseball, sports, and life in general. Remember Coach Scott's purpose with his parody. I thought it was worth sharing here. Here is his end of the season speech to his young team:

The league is giving out participation trophies for the end of the season but given that you managed to lose eleven games this season, the league concluded that you guys didn't even participate. You were just here, on a team so there will be no participation trophies for you this season. They did give us these certificates that basically certify that you were on a team. There is a little blank spot on each one for me to fill out that a player is recognized for something. I tried to fill out something for each of you of what you are recognized for. It was tough but here it is:

- Carter: You are recognized for killing the grass in right field. You never moved. There is a spot out there that should be named after you.
- Jace: You're recognized as the reason Coach Scott started drinking again.
- Othaniel: We saw your name on the draft list and we thought you were Dominican. We thought this kid is going to be good. You showed up to the first

practice and showed us a swing from the Barrio. You are recognized for having a swing from the Barrio.

- Bryce: Your fielding percentage was zero. That's hard to do. You are recognized for having bricks for hands.
- Bubba: All those private lessons didn't pay off, so you are recognized for wasting your parents money on private lessons.
- Chas: You got the most expensive bat on the team, and you still couldn't hit for crap. You are recognized for having the most expensive bat on the team.
- Mason. When I think of what a fart might look like, if you could see a fart, that was what your performance was this season. You are recognized for performance that looked like a physical fart.
- James: Honestly, you didn't do anything this season. I couldn't think of anything, so you are recognized for having skin and teeth and breathing oxygen.
- Steele: You were picked up in a trade from another team for a box of balls. You are recognized for that.
- Memphis: Baseball is not your thing, so you are recognized for having a bright future in the high school band.

Coach Scott concluded the team meeting with, "Thank you and I hope I never see you guys again."

While Bergin's stories are to prove a point, there are instances still where this same humor is present in real mound visit conversations. Still, a lot more in little league but also some in the major leagues.

Rick Wilkens caught 11 seasons in the Major Leagues between 1991 and 2001 for many teams but most with the Chicago Cubs. In fact, when catching for the Braves, he caught Greg Maddux's First Cy Young season. Rick stated that he always went to the mound and cracked a joke to break the 'spell.' He called the 'spell' the pitchers train of thought at that moment that happens with all pitchers. Humor, as we will continually show, is effective in the right situations.

There are many reports and pitcher admissions of a catcher saying something funny to the pitcher at the mound and it ends up usually making them more relaxed. It all depends on the game situation and the pitcher. Some pitchers are high stung, others are more relaxed and looser. Some guys are good at thriving on pressure and challenges; others want a more laid back, relaxed approach.

Let's Talk Pitching (letstalkpitching.com) is a discussion forum for baseball pitchers from former pro pitcher Steven Ellis. Some of the comments by readers on the subject of mound visit conversation have turned up some humorous gems. Typical things said to a pitcher or from a catcher say before the catcher turns around and jogs back to the plate:

"Hey, it's just you and me. I'll call it. You throw it. Let's go!"

"Just nod your head. I'm gonna run back to the plate now. Make me look smart."

"Think about the bullpen before the game. Let's throw like that."

"My legs were getting cramped back there. Let's do this!"

"Throw it right through my mitt. I need a new one anyway."

"If you are done screwing around, let's get this guy."

If a catcher has a humor strategy in mind, they are intent on avoiding talk about mechanics, delivery, or faults. A good catcher, many times, finds something positive or just tries to break the tension before returning to their backstop position. Many catchers report that when things aren't going well, the pitcher is really not in the mood for a therapy session, or on the spot coaching. You really can't fix mechanics on the mound in the middle of a game. That's also a time where humor defuses a lot of situations.

"You know, you'd pitch a lot better with your eyes open…"

"Forget about the girl behind me in the box seats. She's not waving at you."

"That last pitch was a beauty. Right down the middle, then into the parking lot. Here's another baseball. Skipper wants you not to lose this one."

This was kind of funny, but it worked so it's worth sharing.

Catcher: Whatever you do, don't look at second base while we're talking.

Pitcher: Ok.

Catcher: That runner is taking the most ridiculous lead off second that I have ever seen. And your shortstop has been covering the bag each time.

Catcher: Do not turn around to look at him now, or when you come set. Look like you're about to pitch and then do the spin move we practiced a couple weeks ago.

Pitcher: Nods.

Next pitch: The pitcher does not even glance back at second but throws there anyway and picks off the opposing runner by a mile to end the inning. The runner was so surprised, he didn't even try to avoid the tag.

Everyone was happy.

Dusty Baker and Max Scherzer – Funny Mound Visit

Many of these stories are about catcher-pitcher interactions or manager/coach-pitcher interactions. Some of the participants are well known, and some are lesser known. This one is included because both participants are high profile and usually turn out baseball highlights of one type or another. The pitcher is Max Scherzer. His team at the time was the Washington Nationals, managed by Dusty Baker. The game was one of the Washington Nationals against the New York Mets (the team that Scherzer eventually was traded to years later). Almost 42,000 fans at New York's Citi Field witnessed what ended up being a comical exchange between pitcher Scherzer and manager Baker.

There are other stories here with Dusty involved with other pitchers. Dusty represents what many have referred to as the ageless heartbeat of the game. He's been present as part of many historical moments and highlights throughout baseball history. One famous Dusty Bakerism is,

'When you have an opportunity to take the lead and you don't, most of the time something bad happens.' That's part of his management philosophy managing the team or even making mound visits.

Scherzer was pitching a baseball gem. As Larry Brown of larrybrownsports.com (@LBSports), a former nationally syndicated sports radio host at *FOX Sports Radio* and more, reported that in the bottom of the seventh inning of that game, Scherzer was Scherzer and struck out the first two batters. He then walked the next batter. You can guess what happened next with Dusty at the helm. Baker called time and strolled to the pitcher's mound to visit with Max.

Through Chelsea Janes (@chelsea_janes), as reported by Larry Brown, the mound conversation ensued, and the talk quickly turned directly away from the heat of the moment and even baseball and shifted to one about Max's eyes. Most baseball fans know, but if you didn't, when you look at Max, it is immediately obvious, staring you in the face, that he has one brown eye (left) and one blue eye (right). Scherzer has a condition called heterochromia iridium, which means the irises of his eyes are different colors.

Dusty's purpose in that situation was one of more giving Scherzer a breather, a break in the action and as Dusty always says, a chance to reset and refocus. It wasn't a high-pressure conversation. Dusty asked Scherzer, "Which eye you looking out of?"

Scherzer's reply according to reporter, Janes was, "The (freaking) brown one." That's really all Baker needed for that mound visit. He left his pitcher in to proceed. They went on to a 6-1 victory over the Mets.

Later, Scherzer was asked why he told Dusty it was the brown one he was looking out of and he quickly replied in Max Scherzer style, "It's the pitching eye." Dusty knew later that he wouldn't have been able to argue with that. Scherzer liked his share of humor in baseball. It is well known that Max Scherzer had brought a fun, light-hearted atmosphere to the Washington Nationals clubhouse when he joined the club. He tends to be funny when dealing with the media.

Mound Oddities

Kyle Snyder – Injured During a Mound Visit

This is not related to mound visit conversations or behind-the-scenes strategies and coaching but it is related to mound visits and is another oddity and different, so it is included here.

Sports injuries are one of the most common injuries in the modern western world. Almost always, these injuries are related to players and direct participants. Sometimes, not usually, injuries go beyond players.

In an August 2002, game between the Detroit Tigers and the Tampa Bay Rays, the Ray's pitching coach Kyle Snyder came up lame while trotting out for a mound visit with his pitcher Shane McClanahan.

Watching the video of that part of the game shows Kyle popping out of the dugout with a nice trot and took a couple of skips. At the time, no one was sure whether the skips were part of his gleeful trip to the mound or if it was a result of a calf injury that happened in the trot/skip. He couldn't have more than 20 feet from the steps of the dugout. The 44-year-old, 6'7", Snyder had to return to the dugout, and manager Kevin Cash had to take over the mound visit and speak with pitcher McClanahan instead.

"He pulled a calf muscle—pulled it, strained it, popped it—we haven't gotten the final injury report yet," manager Cash reported after the game. He admitted that it was his time 'step up.'

Reporters, fans, and players kidded Snyder and said it might be a lesson that even when you're not an active player in a game, it's always important to stretch before any physical activity. Chalk that up to a mound visit but not a mound visit.

Justin Verlander – No Hitter Mound Visit

A question arose if there are ever any mound visits during a no hitter. The answer is yes. I'm sure there are many situations where the pitcher needs to get back on track, needs a breather or wants to make sure the pitch/game strategy is intact.

Here is one from Houston Astros pitcher (at the time), Justin Verlander when he pitched one of his no hitters.

Justin Verlander was pitching to catcher Robinson Chirinos in a game, late in the season (September 2019) in Toronto, playing the Blue Jays. It might not be a formal title, but Chirinos was considered Verlander's 'personal catcher,' that season. That started in spring training, and they have been batter mates for all of Verlander's starts in 2019. In this case, Chirinos is truly a silent partner.

As reported by Chandler Rome, Astros Beat Writer for the Houston Chronicle, Verlander threw 120 pitches in his game. A single mound visit was made by Chirinos, with two outs in the ninth inning, potentially the last batter. That last batter was power hitter Bo Bichette, probably the toughest out to get in the Blue Jays lineup. Bichette was a recent call up which meant that there was a lack of knowledge by Verlander, related to this hitter. Normally, Verlander uses his mental databank of past experience with batters to attach them in the moment.

Verlander stated after the game, that Bichette was his least favorite person to see at bat. He had only faced him a couple of times earlier in the game. Verlander, being who he is, used that little bit as some confidence in his approach. Not only that little bit of confidence but there was a nugget of intelligence that Verlander and Chirinos noticed and discussed.

Chirinos observed that when Bichette got to a two-strike count, he didn't do a leg kick that was part of his normal swing. Chirinos described it more as a stride. That also led to a shorter swing when he had a two-strike count.

Verlander proceed to pitch to Bichette. Of course, during a potential no hitter, emotions are flying, nerves are on edge and the players and crowd are into every pitch. Verlander, according to him, threw five of his hardest fastballs of that game. He eventually reached a full count with the sixth pitch being fouled back. What followed next? Verlander fooled the hitter with his slider. Bichette hit a chopped hit to third baseman, Abraham Toro who fielded it cleanly and threw to first base for the final out and the completion of the no hitter.

Also as reported by Rome, Chirinos met his pitcher between the mound and home plate, not the most normal spot for a 'mound visit,' but effective, nonetheless. Chirinos was calm. He put his hand on his pitcher's shoulder and started to talk just like he had in any other mound visit in any other game, no hitter or not. Their pitcher-catcher relationship called for the calmness that ensued for a fruitful chat.

Rome reported that after the game, Chirinos said that Verlander called him by name and said how much he appreciated him. Chirinos expressed, "That's the only thing you ask for, and guys, appreciate everything that we do as a catcher like scouting reports, all we do as we prepare for them. Listening to those words meant a lot to me."

As a tribute to his catcher, Verlander stated that the year had been special for the two of them. He was quoted as saying, "Right from the get-go in spring training, catcher Chirinos works his butt off and tries so hard to get on the same page as pitchers and does whatever he can to help us win. I share this with him as much as anyone."

Even muti-Cy Young award winner pitcher, Justin Verlander appreciates his catcher and the timely mound visit even if only once in a no hitter game.

Baseball Confidential Extras

Covering Up of the Face – During Mound Visit Conversations

More and more, if not always, these days you see catchers and coaches visiting the pitcher on mound visits for their conversation and they cover their mouth with their glove. It's as if they think someone is going to read their lips and know what is being discussed. I don't remember this being done, growing up with the game. Fear of lip-reading is exactly the case and reason for the cover ups. When did this start and who did it first? The credit as far as baseball records go, goes to Will Clark who was batting for the San Francisco Giants at Wrigley Field during the 1989 NLCS, against Cubs pitcher, Greg Maddux. The bases were loaded and Cubs manager, Don Zimmer made a mound visit. He wanted to chat with Maddux about what to pitch in this bases loaded situation.

Will Clark, stood in the batter's box waiting, adjusting his batting gloves, taking a few practice swings while at the same time watching the pow wow on the mound. He could clearly see the faces of Zimmer and Maddux. He could almost pick up a few words just by reading their lips. The mound visit was over, and Maddux was ready to pitch. He would up, threw hard and Will Clark proceed to hit a home run of the grand slam variety. High fives all around. After the game, Clark was asked about the at bat and that home run producing pitch. Will Clark, a good fastball hitter, read the lips of Maddux when talking to Zimmer, saying 'fastball.' To a good fastball hitter, if they know one is coming, chances are they will have good luck in their at-bat. Clark had good luck and the practice of mouth covering during mound visits was born. Pitchers, catchers, and coaches today either thank him or blame him.

Handing the Pitcher, the Ball

Jason Turbow describes this very well in *The Baseball Codes*.

Jim Barr was a pitcher for the San Francisco Giants. His manager at the time was the fiery Frank Robinson. Barr, who had a reputation of what has been termed, 'independent thought.' For the record, Frank Robinson had little appreciation for independent thought from players.

Barr was having a semi-challenging inning at Shea Stadium during one 1983 game against the Mets. During the fourth inning of that game, out to the mound trotted manager Robinson. Barr saw it as pitcher's peripheral vision seems to be trained to watch for such things. Barr did not want to be replaced. He was defiant. Barr turned, before Robinson reached the mound and attempted to storm to the dugout, ball in hand. Robinson grabbed the passing pitcher and proceeded to kick into high-intensity manager status. Robinson took Barr back to the mound and Barr continued more antics, getting in the way of the relieving pitcher. Robinson escorted Barr back to the dugout where the intense management conversations continued. Observers only said, "It wasn't a pretty situation."

Jim Barr and Frank Robinson reconciled after that situation. One point here is that a decade later, Barr became pitching coach at Sacramento State University. At the beginning of every season, Barr, the manager, laid out his rules for his team. He likened his rules to those expressed to him by Sparky Anderson. One in particular, reminding him of his situation with Robinson was, "When I visit the mound for a pitching change, I want only for the departing player to give me the ball and walk quietly away, no questions asked." It was time for the pot to call the kettle black and he did.

Frank Robinson, as manager, has had more than one mound situation with pitcher defiance. In 2005, Robinson went to the mound to pull a Nationals pitcher Tomo Ohka. Ohka turned his back to Robinson as the manager walked to the mound in the fourth inning of a game between the Washington Nationals and the Florida Marlins (not yet known as the Miami Marlins). Ohka made as if to hand him the ball, then jerked it back. Robinson then had to grab the ball out of Ohka's hand to make the pitching change.

Ohka stormed off the mound. Robinson just turned and stared after his pitcher; however, the pitcher was eventually fined by the_Nationals for showing disrespect to manager Frank Robinson while being removed from the game.

"He was disrespectful to me," Robinson said. "He had his back to me. I put my hand out for the ball and he didn't give it to me."

General Manager of the Nationals, Jim Bowden reiterated what's been written here, "One thing you can't have on a major league club is have a player show up a manager." Ohka showed up his manager. Written or unwritten rule, that's the rule.

Before the week was out, Ohka was traded away for a player from Milwaukee.

Different Approaches – Reasons for a Mound Visit

Throughout the history of baseball, pitchers, catchers, coaches, and managers will have varying viewpoints about mound visits. Many strategies and approaches are used, agreed with, and disagreed with.

Some will say a visit to a pitcher helps him get back on track. Some use various ways of motivation including reverse psychology. Clearly, though there are the pros and cons of dos and don'ts during a visit to the hill.

There is one school of thought that says going to the mound to talk about the pitcher's delivery or his pitching mechanics is not a good idea and can be counterproductive. On the other side, you have those that say if you pick up the smallest of flaws at the time of delivery, it's worth telling the deliverer, the pitcher. Some pitching coaches don't want their pitchers thinking about mechanics or even changes to that, when on the mound. That type of coaching happens best, between games. Thinking of mechanics may remove the focus of the job at hand and batter for the very next pitch. Small suggestions like, extending yourself or turning your hips is fine but not long conversations about mechanics.

Often a mound visit happens to help a pitcher catch his breath, slow down, establish or re-establish his pace. All kinds of things are in play here. It could be a pitchers rookie appearance, a tense bases loaded situation or something else that sends the adrenaline sky high. A break in the action in the form of a mound visit can help return that adrenaline to earthly levels. Slowing down is not overrated when it comes to pitching. Proper breathing and pace can also support mechanics and delivery as much as mindset.

There are coaches everywhere but in the form of armchair coaches. All feel the pressure and have the advice. No one feels the pressure of a game more than the pitcher himself. He is the first one to say he doesn't want to underperform. That is in head continually. Encouragement, positive words, and pep talks help that. These can all be parts of a mound visit by a catcher, coach, or manager. Pitchers do better for positive catchers and positive managers. Pointing out the positive still works today. We are all human and our mindsets respond to positive reinforcement.

One of the worst things a catcher or coach can say (but it still happens) is, "Just throw strikes." Pitchers know this and don't need this reminder. That is not going to magically produce better pitches in the strike zone. A pitcher doesn't go to the mound and plan to throw bad pitches.

Positive reinforcement works, but so does humor. In *Baseball Confidential*, we review, at length, baseball, and mound visit humor. Humor can be relaxing to a pitcher. A relaxed pitcher will at least have more fun and probably perform better.

These are just a few fundamental approaches, pros and cons, depending on the planned approach and each and every individual. Every pitcher is different. The more a catcher, coach, and manager knows his pitcher, the more productive his mound visit will be.

Herm Winningham – Consummate Reserve

Baseball Confidential is all about talk behind the scenes, communication between players, coaches, and managers. Communication can come in the form of mound visits, locker room meetings, pre-game pep talks, post-game reviews and reprimands and more.

When talking to professional baseball players and asking them about some of their most memorable pre-game pep talks or speeches from the manager or coaches, most say there really weren't as many as people think.

Herm Winningham was a reserve center fielder that played mostly with the Washington Nationals and the Cincinnati Reds. Herm was part of the 1990, wire to wire, World Series Championship team with the Cincinnati Reds. He verified that part about pep talks but did elaborate on in game communication. When describing his day of communication, it was really a description of what goes on in a typical game day, pre-game, and any communication during that. He calls it all 'idiosyncrasies' of the game, the behind-the-scenes talk.

Herm was a reserve player mostly. He knew that he accepted that, that was a clearly defined role on the team and that was fine with all. Usually, the reserves or new and upcoming players would all get to the ballpark early on game day. Their mantra clearly was come early, stay late.

Players would change into their batting practice attire.

Before the game, they would be in a room with infielders or a room with outfielders. Back in Herm's Day, players couldn't rely on, 'notes in the hat,' like you see today. In the pre-game meeting, the head scout would give his report, players would read it, review it, study it and that was it. Asking ball players about that and they would tell you that once reviewing the scouting report, they 'knew how to play them.' They were confident about that. That's about all they had and they made it work.

They then would trot out for a round of batting practice. Come back in afterwards and eat and then go back out for infield or outfield shags, certainly a lot more than done today, according to Herm. After that, players would sign a few autographs and change into their game uniform. After that, there were no more pre-game meetings. Ball players will tell you we are grown men, know what our jobs are, are plenty motivated and don't need a rah-rah speech before the game. I'm sure there are exceptions but that was generally the rule. Players liked to police themselves as much as they could at this level.

Herm, though, was quick to point out that if they weren't playing well or making too many fundamental mistakes, they would be subject to the traditional butt chewing after the game.

During the game, there was always lots of chatter between players, either on the field or in the dugout. Pitcher, Tom Browning, pitching for the Reds would always move his outfielders around. He had lots of communication all around the field, according to Herm.

The talk in the dugout consisted of everything on a players mind: the game going on, where they would eat after the game, what their off-day plans were and who is the next pitcher up they might face. It was a mishmash but effective and very forthcoming. Herm liked to say they were in the game but out of the game. Herm was a bona fide reserve player that didn't start every game but got his share of playing time as a reserve.

Herm talked about always being mentally prepared, always staying one step ahead of the team manager and a step ahead of the opposing manager. They had to be mentally in the game, so when they were called on in a moment's notice, they were ready. If an opposing right hander was in the bullpen warming up, all the reserve left hand batters would disappear to the hitting tunnel to get loose and warmed up, just in case. Reserve players had to be ready, know the situation, who was next up, when a pinch hitter might be needed and more, in the game but not in the game.

Herm shared a couple of reserve player idiosyncrasies. Herm, played for Lou Piniella, manager of the Cincinnati Reds at the time. Lou Piniella was probably the most fiery and passionate manager in the history of the Reds. His message to the team from Day One was he did not come as manager to see the Reds lose.

Herm had experienced a few stretches where he wasn't called on to play. He would visit with his manager in his office to ask what was up, was he in trouble, was he not favored in certain situations or what. Lou Piniella, being

Lou Piniella was just very honest with Herm at that point and says, "I just forgot about you." Nothing like honesty and that sure was Lou.

As a reserve player, not playing every day, he was called on to give regular, starting players a day off. Traditionally, Sundays in the major leagues is getaway day, getting ready to travel for the next week. Reserves would predominantly be called on to play on getaway day. That meant that reserve players took it easy and didn't go out heavily on Saturday night. Herm said it best, when in Chicago, as a reserve player on a Saturday night, "Rush Street bites back."

Herm's 1990 team was the first National League team in the era of 162-game series to go wire-to-wire. The Detroit Tigers—managed by Sparky Anderson, the much-loved, one-time manager of the Big Red Machine—also went wire to wire in the American League in their 1984 World Championship season.

In 1990, during that Reds championship season, things went downhill just a little bit when Ken Griffey Sr was released from the team. Griffey Sr was released in the middle of that championship season, signing with the Seattle Mariners to conclude the season, joining his son Ken Jr.

Not really pep talk related but Griffey Sr did give a message to the team upon his release. His message was, "You better start winning. I've already been to a World Series, and I want you to experience the same." Herm said that jumpstarted the team again and as they say, the rest is history. That team, that year, despite Griffey's release, voted to give Ken Griffey Sr a full World Series share and a championship ring, because of his message and what he meant to that team.

Herm retired from major league baseball and got into coaching. He was a coach at area (Orangeburg, South Carolina) high schools and small college teams. As the manager, Herm would mostly send his pitching coach to the pitcher's mound for mound visits, when needed. If Herm made the trip, as the manager, he took the ball from the pitcher, sent him off the mound and replaced him with a reliever. There were times he would go out to ease the pitcher, tell a joke, and make them laugh or break up the monotony. His message always had the underlying theme of, *don't press too much. I know you are working hard to get to the big leagues, but you are playing a game, the game of baseball. Have fun while doing it.*

His best pitching mound visit story involved his revered manager, Lou Piniella. Danny Jackson was pitching for the Cincinnati Reds and not doing well. According to players he was getting 'shelled.' Jackson was replaced with relief pitcher, Tim Birtsas. At some point, manager Piniella made a mound visit, said his piece, and returned to the dugout. Later in the same inning, Piniella, not intending to replace Birtsas, made another mound visit. Lou had forgotten about mound visit number one that inning. When a manager visits the mound twice in an inning, he has to make a pitching change. When Lou made his second visit, there was no one warming up in the bullpen to come in to replace Birtsas. Lou and team had to scramble to comply with the rules, but it was a funny situation to those involved in the game at the time.

Herm received a great baseball tip (player communication extraordinaire) from Montreal Expos teammate, Jim Wohlford. The Expos were playing the San Diego Padres, in San Diego, really late in the season. The Expos were out of playoff contention. San Diego went on to win the game to clinch their division championship. At the conclusion of the game, there was celebration like one would expect in major league baseball, lots of whooping and hollering. Jim turned to Herm and said, "Sit down and watch this (celebration). This is what you play for." Herm said that tip and scene was forever etched in his mind, very motivating and memorable. He was happy for the opposing team, but it made for a very quiet plane ride on their return to Montreal.

Pre-Game Speeches

Little League World Series coach – Touching pep talk to his pitcher son

A lot of *Baseball Confidential* is related to the professional level of baseball, primarily, the major leagues. There are stories related to minor leagues, college ball and even little league. This is one special mound visit that happened in Little League that makes one wish that all mound visit conversations were picked up by players and coaches wearing mics.

The Little League World Series was in full swing in 2016, when a team from Bend, Oregon was playing a team from Italy. International games, even at this level, are highly competitive and pressure packed even for eleven-, twelve- and thirteen-year-old players.

Twelve-year-old Isiah Bugsy Jensen was on the mound for the Oregon team. It was the fifth inning, and an Italian power hitter was coming to bat. Bugsy, the Bend team pitcher needed one more out to get out of a tense inning. Jensen was pitching a great game but in the top of the fifth inning fatigue sets in. It was obvious that Bugsy was starting to struggle. At age twelve, this is the only thing that matters in the whole world. Anyone watching knew how the pitcher was feeling. Bugsy finished to the batter up and ended up walking him.

Out of the dugout, came his coach for a mound visit and ensuing pep talk. That coach just happened to be Bugsy's father, Coach Joel Jensen.

What followed was one of the most touching father-son/player conversations you'll ever hear in a baseball game of any type.

Here is how that conversation, from the dad/coach went:

"I just came out to tell you how much I love you as a dad and a player. You're doing awesome out here. One more hitter and I'm going to duke (the warmed-up, bullpen, relief pitcher in waiting). This is your last hitter. Ok? You understand? Come right after them. Cheer up, have some fun, go right after him."

I'm not sure that you would hear that exact conversation in a major league mound visit but it was certainly one that fit the mission of Little League Baseball.

Little League Baseball's mission statement reads as follows:

"Little League Baseball is a non-profit organization to help and voluntarily assist young boys and girls in developing the qualities of citizenship, discipline, teamwork, and physical well-being through the medium of baseball and softball with guidance and exemplary leadership. By espousing the virtues of character, courage and loyalty, the Little League program is designed to develop superior citizens rather than superior athletes."

The father/son/player conversation was a shining example of this mission in action. That's why there is a great track record of today's major league ball players who once played in Little League Baseball.

Pitcher Bugsy ended up striking out his one more batter and the team from Bend, Oregon went on to win the game. Chalk it up to a successful mound visit and a little bit of fatherly advice.

This story is a true reminder of sports teaching life lessons.

Albert Pujols-Pre-Game Speeches – Memorable and Relevant

Baseball Confidential has stated that any good sports fan wants to know what is said on the mound, in the locker room, behind closed doors and more. Pitchers, catchers, coaches, managers, and other players have given us perspectives on the behind the scenes, somewhat confidential, communication that happens in the great game of baseball. With this exposure to coaches, players, and managers *Baseball Confidential* is bringing much of that to light.

Two of these communication points are the pre- and post-game speech. They absolutely vary greatly, in delivery, content, length, purpose and more.

Some will say that many of these types of 'speeches,' are repetitive. Some have told me that once you hear one you have heard them all. We will dispel that here. Sure, there are many cliches used when trying to communicate and mostly, to motivate a team.

Sometimes, in a game, depending on the point in the season, the success of the season and the next hurdle to be tackled, during a season, teams and players need a rally cry in the form of an inspiring, moving locker room speech.

Appeals and encouragement to try harder helps many athletes to reach an optimal level of awakening and eventual performance, but care must be taken to not cause others to become over stimulated beyond focus. After all, a pep talk is communication that a player can use to understand and eventually process different situations, scenarios, and obstacles.

Some of the best athletes don't need any outside influential motivation as they rely on their own self-motivation. It has been found that it sure can't hurt to still have an outside motivational influence in a locker room. This is very true at the little league, high school, and college levels where there are no gigantic pay checks to inspire players.

A pre-game pep talk can help a player feel more courageous, bold, productive, or pumped up and enthusiastic. This also works for self-coaching. Some of the best pep talks are given by and to individuals, themselves. A person knows what we are capable of, better than anyone else; however, outside motivations help and work.

The motivating pep-talk, locker room speech is almost a tried-and-true sports tradition. It is very common in locker rooms at all levels. At the end of the day, there is nothing more motivating than success. Seeing players high fiving, cheering, toasting, and piling up as a result of not only their performance but of their motivation is part of what sports are all about.

Let's look at a few specific moments captured in the spirit of motivation.

Perennial All-Star and future Hall of Famer, Albert Pujols played his last season in 2022. In that he was chosen for the 2022 All-Star Game. Before the game, he took the locker room opportunity to thank the players from all different teams. His speech of thanks was moving, inspirational, emotional, and memorable, all the things that a good pre-game speech should be.

MLB Network tweeted out the entire speech which resulted in a locker room standing ovation from his fellow National League All-Stars.

Pujols' speech was more thankful but there were pieces that were very motivational, especially for newer and younger players. After he was done, most were inspired to run through brick walls for Albert Pujols. I will borrow from the MLB tweet and share this excerpt of Pujols' speech:

"For me, it's an honor to be here. And just looking around, my last year of my career, it has been an amazing career…

"We come together for two days. We compete during the course of the season, but we come together for two days and have fun, enjoy just talking. My last year just being here in the All-Star Game and seeing future Hall of Famers, and managers of the year and championship players…And the young talent there is in this game. Twenty-two freaking years in this game is a long time for myself. I think it's time to walk out. But it's just a true honor to be here and I'm enjoying every single moment, every single minute of this over the last couple of days. Obviously, tomorrow we're going to wake up and go on our way, but thank you so much, guys. Thank you so much for the memories...

"Yesterday was really special to me. Somebody asked me, 'What do you think about that moment yesterday when the players came over and embraced you?' To me, it's probably going to be one of the top moments of my career. And I'm serious, guys. Twenty-two years in this game and yesterday was really emotional...

"As you know, we're going to go out there and have fun, the All-Star Game is about having fun. Enjoy it. But remember that jersey that you represent. Who you represent when you take that field. Don't take anything for granted. Play the game hard. And let's go kick some butt. Let's go get a win and try to enjoy it. So, thank you so much, guys, I wish you all the best in the second half except when you play against the Cardinals. So, God bless you, guys, and thank you so much. It means a lot."

That locker room moment was more for many players than those baseball players come to expect.

Some of this motivation and inspiration works and has an effect, but most is gone the moment the game actually starts. By the first pitch, the first out, the first hit, things are back to normal mindsets and players forget that speech in the locker room. That's normally the case. In the case of Albert Pujols, his speech might be the exception.

Pre-game speeches take many forms. There are those that are thankful, emotional, and motivating like the Pujols delivery. There are others that are rants, yelling, Theory X management styles or otherwise.

Chipper Jones-Post-Game Speeches – Memorable and Relevant

Sometimes, pre-game speeches are done to provide focus. Sometimes, they are to laser pinpoint things to pay attention to. Other times, they can be a divergence used to relax and bring a team together. The latter was the case or something close to it during Chipper Jones 2012 All-Star Game speech in his locker room before the mixed team spilled out for the game.

As in every All-Star Game, there are many story lines regarding players, teams, and the game itself. This game was Chipper Jones' final All-Star appearance. He knew it and his teammates knew it. It was only fitting then that he gives the pre-game pep talk, especially with the number of younger players present. Have a listen (remember sometimes pre-game speeches by team leaders are a divergence used to relax, bring a team together and create another memory for all):

"Guys, listen. I'm looking around this room, and I see that not all of us have chairs. The team that wins this game is going to be awarded plenty of chairs. It's important to have things to sit on, such as a chair. By the end of this game, people are going to say, 'Bryan LaHair? More like Bryan LaChair, on account of the chair he is sitting in. That is a joke I made.' That is a joke a made-up person made. That's why we need to go out and win this thing. Chairs. Chairs are comfortable and important.

"Ok, guys, let's get to the dugout. There are places to sit there. You may be asked to briefly play baseball, but playing baseball is more similar to the experience of sitting in a chair than any other sport, including cycling. Chairs, et cetera. Sincerely, Chairper Jchairnes."

Whether it was Chipper's speech or him ending the game with a hit, his National League went on to an 8-0 victory.

Hideki Matsui-Post-Game Speeches – Memorable and Relevant

I first heard of Luis 'Squeegee' Castillo, as he is considered the most famous bat boy in the history of Major League Baseball. Luis was born in the Bronx and grew up idolizing the New York Yankees. As a teenager, he was the Yankees' bat boy between the 1998 and 2005 seasons. In his book, Clubhouse Confidential – a behind closed doors look at the New York Yankees from the perspective of a bat boy who saw it all, Castillo revealed a story about Hideki Matsui's pre-game message to his team before Game Seven of the 2004 ALCS.

The Boston Red Sox had a very good season in 2004. Their most historical feat was when they defeated the New York Yankees in four games of the seven-game series, to take the series, after losing the first three games. They are the only team to win the ALCS after a 3-0 deficit.

Luis was in the right position at the right time and heard the exact conversations between the then-Yankees manager Joe Torre and designated hitter Hideki Matsui. Per Castillo, when Torre asked Hideki what the plan was for Game Seven, the Yankees slugger replied with some attitude. Perhaps that attitude was also a portrayal of a bit over confidence. Hideki was poignant but the team lost the game and series. (Boston went on to win the World Series that year).

Hideki's words were brief. Here is what Castillo overheard:

Hideki: "Kick A*. Pop Champagne. And Get Some H*'s." It never quite came out what the h*'s meant but Hideki knew and delivered it convincingly.

Little did Hideki know at that time of his one-line speech, that the Red Sox would not only seize the ALCS from the New York Yankees, but they would also go on to win the World Series that year. It was a memorable year for the Boston Red Sox and probably a lesson for the Yankees of not being over optimistic.

Casey Stengel – Simple and Masterful Pre-Game Message

Sometimes, pre-game speeches can take the simplest of forms. It's usually a function of the situation and the person who is delivering the message.

Unless you have been living under the proverbial baseball rock, you've heard of Casey Stengel. Stengel is best known as the manager of the championship New York Yankees of the 1950s and later, the expansion New York Mets. Casey Stengel had 54 unenviable years in baseball. Casey saw, lived, and played during the Dead Ball Era. He also was a teammate of Mickey Mantle who blasted home run after home run.

Spark Anderson said of Casey, "Casey Stengel knew his baseball. He only made it look like he was fooling around. He knew every move that was ever invented and some that we haven't even caught on to yet."

As told in the book, *Yogi: A Life Behind the Mask by Jon Pessah*: "It's moments before Game Four when Berra hears Stengel call the team together in the locker room. Yogi has rarely heard Casey give a pregame speech, but the Yankees have looked listless while losing two of the first three games to a Giants team they all think they should beat. 'Fellas, I just want to mention one thing to you,' Casey says, showing little emotion. 'You are not playing these guys 22 games – you only have four left to play. What the hell are you going to do, let them run you out of the ballpark'?"

Pessah goes on to say in his book, "Stengel looks at every group of players standing around him, letting his words sink in, and says simply, 'Okay, let's go.' Raschi, Reynolds, and Lopat dominate the Giants in the next three games. Yankee hitter's pound out 23 runs, and Stengel's team sweeps the next three games to secure their place in history with their third straight title."

That's Casey Stengel, that's the Yankees, and that's baseball.

Post-Game Speeches

University of Texas Baseball Coach – Loud, Ranting, Emotional Post Game Speech

I reviewed many post-game and pre-game speech recordings. I've included some in *Baseball Confidential*. There was one that stood out to me that I didn't include. It was an absolute tirade by a University of Texas head baseball coach after a sloppy game. The post-game speech was full of swear words, belligerent and loud-mouthed rantings, emotional confrontation and more. If I was the recipient and I know many that agree, this type of delivery would fall on deaf ears, despite the volume and inflections. While that is my opinion, there are others who believe differently. I viewed this video on *TikTok*. The reason I am including here is to share with you the wide range of comments to show the varied opinions on whether a speech like this works or doesn't.

(To view the rant, search on TikTok: Texas baseball coach locker room speech by Pana Productions. I will not include it here.)

Here are the comments on the speech (quoted and un-edited from the TikTok post):

- Some of us appreciate tough coaching styles more than others…
- The coaches I've had over the past few years have been soft. I hope I have a coach like this one day.
- You need a coach like this who sincerely cares about his team performing well. This is the type of coach I would like.
- It worked! The team then went on a huge multi-game win streak and made the College World Series.
- The Bobby Knight of college baseball.
- The man was a fantastic coach.
- Kids these days would be looking for their safe place.
- This was over the top intentionally. He felt they needed an abrupt wakeup call so he delivered it.
- Hmmm. It's just a game.
- Bring the heat coach.
- He seems upset.
- Love him. RIP Coach.
- That's a coach right there, wish all of 'em were like this, the world would be a better place.
- Love it. Kids today need a lot of this.
- This method isn't sustainable. It works here and there but eventually players are just like here he goes again.

These are unedited comments and there were more. This is just to show the varying viewpoints of such a (in my opinion) caustic rant. I wanted to share it because different types of coach communication affect players differently. It's all a function personality, values, up-bringing, inherent talent and more. These comments show that it affects people differently.

Justin Verlander Post-Game Speech – Memorable and Relevant

Whether it's a mound visit, a pre-game speech or a post-game cheer, Justin Verlander's name often comes up. It was 19 September 2022, and the Houston Astros just clinched the AL West after a victory over the Tampa Bay Rays at the Rays home park, Tropicana Field.

With a clinching comes a champagne party in the locker room. With a champagne party usually comes a congratulatory, rallying speech, especially with another step left on the way to play for the World Series championship. That type of speech is usually by the leader, in this case, manager Dusty Baker. Dusty, in Dusty fashion, decided to exercise his team building attitude and delegate the speech to one of his player team leaders. Dusty asked seasoned vet and pitching rock star, Justin Verlander to say a few words.

Verlander is pretty good at following directions, so he took the podium (a table full of the bubbly ready to be broken out) and said his few words. Sometimes, the best messages are short and sweet or at least short. Verlander took 30 seconds to pepper his impromptu speech with words that included what you would guess would replace the word, 'freaking' in his brief rant:

"Being gone for the last couple years, guys, it just really puts things into perspective. These moments, even though we expected to be here, don't take these little things for granted, man. This is (freaking) awesome to win. Your (freaking) division is not easy at this (freaking) level. I know we got bigger things in sight, but let's (freaking) enjoy this (freaking) moment."

The emotions, facial expressions and voice were all on full display.

Justin Verlander was a valuable teammate to all those he played with when with the Detroit Tigers. The same can now be seen with his newer team (at the time). The Houston Astros values him just the same. That short and sweet speech continues that respect and comraderies that personifies Justin Verlander.

Michael Brantley – Post - Game Speeches – Memorable and Relevant

The pre-game chat is inspirational and motivational but really, it is a message to get players do something good, something better, and something exceptional, all toward a common goal. Post-game speeches can have the same effect.

All-Star and World Champion Michael Brantley took the lead to talk to his team to encourage and influence them at probably the right time. His post-game speech is credited for shifting the 2022 World Series for the Houston Astros at just the right time.

Brantley's speech came after Game Three of the series against the Philadelphia Phillies. The Astros lost that game, 7-0. The Phillies blasted five home runs to send their signal that they were for real. After this Game Three, they were down 2-1 in the best of seven World Series.

Brantley was a seasoned vet. He could tell that some of his teammates were down in the dumps after that. At those moments, players are uncertain and sometimes, lay down and wilt. Brantley is not one, usually, to be in the spotlight, especially in the locker room. This night was different.

Michael stood up in front of the whole team and gave them his two cents worth of what needed to happen for them to capture the Commissioner's Trophy for that World Series.

The younger players and specifically, David Hensley told Chris Baldwin, journalist for *Paper City Magazine*, "he told us that we needed to keep believing, to keep playing the way we can play. To keep going. He told us to forget about worrying about losing. To just keep playing our game."

There was more to it than just that, but it worked. The Astros did not lose another game in the series after that speech. Maybe that speech is what inspired the no-hit game against the Phillies the following night. One never knows the power of those simple speeches.

Brantley went on to say, "I just saw us kind of down. I wanted to remind each and every one of my teammates how special this team is and that we're not letting this one slip away." That's all it took. That's one of those behind-the-scenes speeches that are credited to him to help change things, even if it's just mindset. Mindset changes work just as well.

Teammate Lance McCullers said that talk meant a lot.

Astros right fielder, Kyle Tucker said, "he told us it's just not over. That we've got to keep our foot on the gas and keep going. It doesn't matter if we're up or down, we got to keep pushing and keep putting together good at-bats. Together, as we can."

Tucker said parts of that speech became the Astros battle cry all the way to victory: "This is ours. We've just got to go get it."

Brantley finished his time in the locker room spotlight by expressing, "This is a special opportunity, and we can celebrate this for the rest of our lives. And all we've got to do is play our brand of baseball. And get back to what we do well."

Michael Brantley's simple message caused his team to respond, all the way to the victory podium and champagne party in that locker room, as baseball's World Series Champions.

Conclusion

Baseball Confidential – Conclusion

I now put my eight-year-old hat on and think back to my first major league game. I wondered what players talked about, what was said on mound visits, what the relationships were like, how coaches coach, and more. *Baseball Confidential* has answered those wonderments.

I played sandlot ball; I watched hundreds of games on TV or live. It was fun to watch and learn about the competitiveness that increased as time went on and I became more of an experienced fan. I learned about strategies. I learned about plays. I learned about players, and I learned what it was like to be a player more. *Baseball Confidential* takes that even up a notch.

I learned throughout and especially now that there are so many things that go on with each pitch, with each situation in each part of each game. It truly affirmed for me that this is a great game and passion. I'll say that again. Baseball is a great game and a great passion to have.

Baseball Confidential has offered more about the game within the game. Now hearing from coaches, players, and managers gives even more to watch. Blink and you miss things. By not understanding the behind-the-scenes communication you miss things.

So, besides *Baseball Confidential*, here are more takeaways that can fuel your passion:

- Managers play a chess game. Every move has a purpose and potential consequence. The goal is to win the chess game.
- This sport is based on traditions that are witnessed and/or passed on from generation to generation. Memories stand out from yesterday, today and will continue tomorrow.
- Baseball is full of personalities, storylines, and events that unfold each and every season.
- With the goal of winning, there is a tremendous balance between individual achievement and overall team performance.
- Baseball stays a game from when you are eight years old to present-day adulthood. Boys will be boys. Men will be boys.

As *Baseball Confidential* started with that first trip to the ballpark, it evolved into total experiences and is true fuel to get to that next game.

The game doesn't end with an expired time clock. It ends with the last pitch of the game regardless of the time.

There are so many ways to enjoy the game and to exercise the passion. You can watch games, listen to games, talk about games, read baseball books, review game and player statistics, and participate in the sport in your own way. Maybe it's playing catch or hitting balls in a batting machine. Getting autographs and keeping your own scorecards contribute as well to the passion.

Now that we have ducked behind the scenes and pulled the curtain back for a look at the game, it is our hope that your interest in baseball and feelings about baseball mean that much more. It means more for me, and I hope it will for you. Thank you for reading *Baseball Confidential*.